GW00481080

FOREWORD BY JOHN PAUL DEJORIA

THE MEANING OF LIFE
ACCORDING TO BIKERS

THE BIKER BOOK FOR CHARITY

Schiffer Publishing Ltd®

4880 Lower Valley Road • Atglen, PA 19310

Edited and Introduced by Louise Lewis

Dedicated to the charitable heart of the motorcycle community and to the Spirit that supports and guides my every step.

Courtesy of Sturgis Buffalo Chip Campground

CONTENTS

FOREWORD

Louise Lewis did an exceptional job over the years putting together *The Biker Book for Charity*. We live in a world sometimes of illusion. We see things that sometimes we think are real, yet sometimes they are not. This is one of my favorite sayings. In the world of bikers, many people associate a "biker" with the biker of the past, the one stereotyped in television or movies who just got into trouble. More and more today, we see people who do not get into trouble, but who realize that when you are on your motorcycle and you go driving down the road, especially in the hills and open space, you are grounded to the earth. It is you, the machine underneath you, and the earth all around you. It really grounds you.

I have found that people in this community are the most giving human beings on the planet. Whether it is the Peace, Love & Happiness Ride in Austin, Texas, the one we do in Sturgis for military veterans, or the one we do on the West Coast, the people participating are everyone from the local person working in a motorcycle shop to executives who lead major corporations, and they all just love the open road and love giving back.

I think bikers are some of the most charitable people on the planet. They seem to really care about things other than just themselves. They love our land, they love our country, they love the world, and they love helping others. The biker community is a great community that should be exposed, and I think this is a book that every person should read to learn what the biker community is really all about. Great job, Louise!

Peace, Love & Happiness,

John Paul DeJoria
Biker. Sturgis Hall of Fame & Museum Awardee.
Founder of Patron Spirit, John Paul Mitchell Systems, and John Paul Pet

INTRODUCTION

The Sick Little Boy and the Biker Dude

Today is Christmas Eve. The sky is blue with puffy white clouds. The air is a balmy seventy degrees. A typical winter's day in Southern California. It is also the day of the annual toy run at the children's hospital. Although I have volunteered here for almost two years now, this is my first opportunity to bear witness to the magic that is about to unfold.

For over twenty years, a local H.O.G. (Harley Owners Group) chapter has dedicated Christmas Eve to putting smiles on kids' faces by rolling onto the hospital grounds with an eye-popping array of toys, games, and stuffed animals. My job is to escort the kids—those who got permission from their nurses—outside onto the sunny lawn. All morning long the kids ask: "When are the biker dudes coming? What are the biker dudes gonna bring me? Can I sit on a biker's bike?"

With help from other volunteers, sick children from ages two to fourteen stream slowly out of the hospital—some in wheelchairs, some pulling along their IV poles, and others clutching the hands of the nearest adults. They know that in a few minutes more than one hundred motorcyclists on super-shiny machines will roll deafeningly through the parking lot bearing gifts just for them.

The kids jockey for the best viewing positions, with some sitting cross-legged or squatting on the grass, while others are lucky enough to find some folding chairs set up for the occasion. Happy to escape the confines of their small hospital rooms, they wait restlessly, faces aglow with anticipation and wonder. Minutes go by. Then excitement crackles in the air as the muffled roar of motorcycles is heard down the road. A traffic light turns green and a cavalry of bikes barrel through the intersection, revving their engines to the delight of the kids. "It's the biker dudes!" screams someone in the crowd. "Yay! They're here!"

This yelling onlooker happens to be *me*!

Surveying the crowd, I see that some of the children are stranded behind others, craning their necks to see what is going on. Others, absent of family or friends to share the day, shy away from the big noise and hug the walls of the building, far from the action.

Oh, this will not do! I grab some kids' hands and poke through the crowd, prodding adults out of the way and leading the bewildered youngsters to front-row views. Several wary children are now close enough to actually feel the heat from the engines blasting past.

Two by two, row after row, bikes of all shapes and colors roll by. Men on bikes. Women on bikes. Men and women on bikes and trikes. Decked-out Santas wave and smile at the small fries in their jammies, bandages, hospital gowns, and rolling IV units.

The deafening roar finally subsides as the last of the bikers rumbles into the parking lot and the bikes are shut off. Now the procession to the toy bins begins. There are four big, empty containers already waiting along the wall of the hospital, behind the kids. The bikers head over to the bins and begin filling them to the brim with the colorful bounty they have brought. Watching each rider, the kids quickly check out every toy that drifts past them, eyeballing which one they might want.

I stroll through the crowd, making sure each child is okay. Warm enough? Need a chair? Did you see the cool bikes? Wanna sit on one? As I make my way through, there he is: a fragile little boy in his hospital PJs, maybe five or six years old, sitting all alone, with his little legs dangling over the edge of his chair. Although sullen, he seems aware

of his surroundings, yet at the same time he's oblivious. I am sure being a patient gives him more pressing things to think about than bikers and toys. Or does it? Instantly my heart opens to him.

As I approach the little munchkin, from the corner of my eye I notice a badass-looking biker dude is also headed his way.

I mean no disrespect when I refer to this man, but he is fully decked out as the hardcore stereotype of "the Biker." Had I been casting a biker movie, this guy would be called back on the first day, and he would not need any help from the wardrobe department. He has the do-rag on his head and a long, straggly, graying beard. Faded tattoos march up and down both arms. Worn leather chaps and vest. A chunky metal chain strung from his belt to his back pocket. The classic, weathered, *Easy Rider* boots. He is the complete picture, the real deal.

I make way for the biker to approach the little boy. After all, this gentleman is a participant in the toy run, and he's part of the reason the kids have something to look forward to this Christmas Eve. The boy is well aware of the approaching man and eyeballs him up and down. I am nervous. This little boy looks very unsure of himself, and I'm worried that the man is going to intimidate him. This could end in disaster, or at least tears. As the biker takes another step toward him, I look in the little boy's eyes, which are growing wider as an "oh my God!" expression spreads across his face. With each step by the biker dude, the little boy leans farther and farther back in his chair.

Then I turn toward the man and gaze into his eyes. *Well, I'll be damned. Would you look at that!* There is as much fear in the biker dude's eyes as there is on the face of the sick little boy. Is he simply preparing himself in case the boy freaks out and starts crying? Two boys: one big, one small, and each afraid of the other. *This I've got to see.* I don't move a muscle, and I breathlessly wait to see how this plays out.

Slowing his steps, the man stops within arm's length, crouches down to eye level with the boy, and shakily extends a teddy bear. Well, that is all it takes. With one look at that teddy bear, the sick little boy turns into a regular little kid. He looks up at the biker and gives him the toothiest smile I have ever seen. The dude's face flushes with relief and joy. And in that moment, these two boys become one. With the gift of a simple teddy bear, all fear vanishes.

In the middle of a crowded parking lot filled with kids, bikes, and riders milling around, the little boy is smiling, the biker dude is smiling, and I am crying like a baby. As I wipe away the tears, I hear God say *Your next book is on bikers*. I reply: *Okay*.

In this moment, I learn a simple truth about these folks who straddle a "wild thang." Behind their don't-fuck-with-me masks, this tough-looking crowd is truly a bunch of loving teddy bears with big-ass hearts.

Witnessing that awesome encounter between the sick little boy and the biker dude opened my eyes and, dare I say, opened my mind as well. Deeply moved by that moment, I felt I had been let in on a major secret—these riders are really special people. I was now damned curious to learn what goes on in their heads. And to share my findings with the world.

It seemed only appropriate, if not obvious, that since this book began at a children's hospital, it should be used to help youngsters. And as I learn more about the charitable heart of the motorcycle community, I see just how generous bikers really are: holding thousands of charity rides and other events every year for every cause under the sun. Surveys show that riders give to charity and participate in charitable causes far more than non-riders do, dedicating entire rides to feed the hungry, provide for veterans, aid in cancer research, and, yes, to brighten the lives of children in need.

Join me in celebrating this amazing community that continually gives back and provides a charitable example for all to follow.

CHAPTER ONE

LIFE ITSELF

Life can be many things: To be alive is one of the more positive meanings of the word "life," versus the very negative meaning of life, which is to do life. To live your life happily would be considered to be having a life, versus living a sad life, which would be better described as existing, not living. To be full of life describes an energetic, happy person, in contrast to a low life, which describes a dull, unattractive existence.

The life you live is largely a result of your outlook and the actions you take, so make the best choices and get a life so that you can live a long and happy life.

Rusty Coones—biker, actor (*Sons of Anarchy*), owner of
    Illusion Motorsports, and founder and lead guitar
        for Attika7

Rusty Coones
Courtesy of Robert John Photography

Courtesy of Sturgis Buffalo Chip Campground

Life is everything: spiritual, physical, still. Parts are easy to describe and parts you cannot describe at all. It is impacted by everything we have touched, as well as everyone we touch. The things we have done and the things we look forward to doing.

Roger Allen—carpet cleaner

Stay healthy to an old age.

Robert Conner—school district employee

The meaning of life is the exhaustion of passion and the beginning of wisdom, meaning that when we exhaust all the wonderful things on Earth, we become very wise. Life is a passionate moment. Yesterday is history; tomorrow is the future. Today is a gift—that is why it is called the present.

Dan Haggerty (1942–2016)—actor (*The Life and Times of Grizzly Adams*)

Live life as you see fit and maybe help a few folks along the way. Learn and retain as much as you can so that you don't make the same mistakes the next time around.

Jim Rushing—automotive worker

It is a grand life, if you do not weaken.

Mark Carstensen—mayor of Sturgis, South Dakota

The meaning of life is very simple. It comes down to the two most important days in your life: the day you were born and the day you discover why you were born. February 7, 1961, and July 31, 1982—my birthday, and the day I took the oath to support and defend the US Constitution, commissioned as an Army officer, a **Guardian of the Republic.**

Allen West—Lt. Col., US Army (Ret.); political commentator; and former US Congressman

Allen West

Courtesy of Lt. Col. Allen B. West, US Army (Ret.)

Andy Bandlord
Courtesy of Andy "Bandlord" Bissell

Life is a collection of adventures, challenges, truths, deceptions, loves, and songs—all memorable. Life is about acceptance or denial of the good and the bad in every choice you have ever made. Life's journeys—whether walking or riding—take you to the places and people that continuously define you. Therefore, the meaning of life is a collection of individual defining memories.

Andy "Bandlord" Bissell—musician and writer

To live with love, compassion, and awe. To learn, share, enjoy, give, take, and appreciate. To care for our earth, be tolerant, and be the best human you can be.

Dave Carthey—retired

Life is a form of existence through physical, mental, and spiritual aspects. The owner of the three forms of existence has choices about how they go through life. Their actions will affect others either intentionally or unintentionally. We are designed to interact with others, to make them better. A life that made a difference in someone else's life is a goal attained by our Creator.

Kevin L. Corcoran—director of research and development

Just live. Get out and enjoy all that life has to offer, and that includes riding and exploring this big, beautiful world. And just stay on the roller coaster until life kicks you off.

Doug & Hazel Walker—sales manager; real estate

Life begins with thinking of how to impress your parents. Somewhere along the line, it transcends to: Who am I and where am I going? Then it becomes: How do I help the people I have created to become healthy, happy, and successful teens, adults, and citizens who have aspiration to better themselves and do good for others as well?

Scott Weiland (1967–2015)—former lead singer for rock groups Stone Temple Pilots and Velvet Revolver

To be able to look back at it one day and say: "Damn, that was an entertaining ride."

Riki Rachtman—TV and radio personality

Courtesy of ©Olivier de Vaulx / www.odvphoto.com

Seize each and every day because I'm here for the ride of a lifetime.

Chris Salgardo—brand ambassador of Kiehl's and the host of the Kiehl's LifeRide for amfAR

Chris Salgardo
Courtesy of Travis Shinn

Having seen death in all forms imaginable, it has simply reinforced the awesome, yet temporary, gift we have been given by our Creator. Our time here should be driven by an interest in all that we have been given—free will and the freedom to choose how we invest our time and energies. Life is enhanced by our interactions with our fellow man, as well as our animal friends. We all should recognize that we share a finite place in the history of this earth. Any wisdom we are able to develop should be shared with family, friends, and community.

Jim Blaylock—retired police officer

Value every life. Our organization, Riders for Health, has a goal, and that is to make sure that no one living in rural Africa dies of easily preventable and curable diseases simply because they cannot be reached. Just one trained, local health worker riding a properly maintained motorcycle can take vital health care—day in and day out—to people in desperate need. It doesn't matter how harsh the terrain or how remote the community, the motorcycles and the health care will get through.

Andrea Coleman—founding member of Two Wheels for Life and Riders for Health

To know what meaning can be derived from life, know what it is to die first.

David Uhl—artist, first licensed oil painter for Harley-Davidson

To learn to accept life, accept change, and trust. Never give up on your dreams no matter what anyone says. Your destiny will be determined not by any man, but by you and your relationship to the connected whole within yourself that connects us all. Instinct. Love yourself, your little child within.

Kenny Johnson—actor (*S.W.A.T.*, *Bates Motel*, *Sons of Anarchy*)

Realizing how short life is and how to make the most of it for those on the journey with you. As Jesse Colin Young (the Youngbloods) once sang, "We are but a moment's sunlight, fading in the grass."

Walt Gray—news anchor with ABC10, Sacramento, California

Since my parents passed, my outlook on life has changed. I bought a Harley on my youngest son's eighteenth birthday. After four kids and no problems, it is my turn to enjoy life. Life is so fragile, and everybody takes it for granted until you have a problem as minor as a cold to a major or minor operation. People suddenly realize health is the greatest gift. I am sixty years old this year, and my lifestyle is as if I was sixteen. I surf, ride a Harley, and dance every dance at a party.

Love and appreciate every day. My mother, after suffering three heart attacks, would always say: "Another day in paradise!" I say this every morning when greeting people. If they respond in a negative tone, I share with them the reason why I say it.

Gary Warren—subcontract administrator

The meaning of life for me is how you can look into your heart and believe that life itself is worth living.

Gilles Marini—film and TV actor (*Devious Maids*, *Sex and the City*, *Dancing with the Stars*)

Gilles Marini
Courtesy of Travis Shinn

From the moment of our birth we are dealt a hand of circumstances. The path of life is about challenge and how we meet those challenges. Is this path determined by fate or merely choice? No one has a definitive answer, but one thing is sure: Our decisions determine our success or failure, and how that success or failure affects the world around us. Our legacy is not determined by the things we leave behind, but rather the quality of the lives we have touched.

Melanie Coy—canine legislative advocate

Be true to yourself so you can be true to others. Give respect so you can receive it back. Help others when you can, and expect nothing but a "thank you" in return. Life is too short to be unhappy. Laugh as much as possible and, hopefully, you can make others laugh, too. Make sure you feel good about yourself when you close your eyes at the end of the day.

Stacy Bianco—durable medical equipment manager
and pharmacy clerk

Courtesy of Serenity Cycle Works

Live out all of your dreams and aspirations and accomplish what you can while you are here on Earth. The dream I am living out right now is being an American airman.

Calvin Charles—operation and readiness superintendent

I have been through hell, and there they know me all too well. I want to stop there, just for a while; then I say to myself: "No, not today; I am on a mission." As the evil ways start to bring me down to the fire pits, I say to myself: "Not today or even next week." Now, as I head there even faster and they are all laughing at me from hell, I leave that place and I say: "Not ever again." It was a long battle through hell, but I made it out. And running down the road of life, I see a long bridge to cross, but this time it is different. This time, as it is the true bridge of life, I stop for a minute and look where I have been and where I am going and wonder, "What if?" And also maybe, just maybe, I do have the best life ever and I have a grandson to tell about it.

James Gadsby—laborer

It is more than a heartbeat or lungs breathing in air. It is about one's concern for his fellow brother or sister in this crazy world. It is about the compassion and the understanding that we have for mankind. It is about the care and well-being that we show to all animals, big and small. To be there for when another needs someone. To have fellow human beings know that you will be there through thick and thin, no matter what the situation. To be able to see the beauty in everything and everyone.

Susan Eileen Major West—pediatric private-duty nurse

Every day you get the opportunity to prove who you really are.

Joseph Onesto—real-estate broker

The meaning of life is to have a wide variety of experiences, learn from them, and use them to leave the world a better place than when you entered it.

Matt DiRito—bassist for Pop Evil, founder of Star Treatments

To be alive means to exist in this worldly plane where all living organisms are connected to one another. To live is to successfully exist peacefully among all these living organisms. We are all tied, we are all connected, and we must love, appreciate, and take care of each other. The more good you do, the more good will come to you. Life is tough, extremely hard at times, and something you will never make it through alive, but your legacy will live forever. Know that when you are doing good, your heart will be the fullest it will ever be. Don't look for the meaning in life; make your life meaningful.

Cindy Snow—tax preparer and executive vice president of Bikers Overseeing Living Dependents (B.O.L.D.)

Basically, everyone has a journey to travel, and it is up to you how much of the scenery you take in and how far you go. The falls and wrecks are a part of life and not anything to be afraid of, only a reminder that the ground will always be there to catch you.

Stay true and be your creative self. You can't get yesterday back. Forgive those who have wronged you, and forgive yourself. Listen to your thoughts more than you listen to others, and be open to change. Everyone you meet in life is for a reason. It is up to you to figure out the lesson.

Rod Abraham—motorcycle mechanic and veteran

Life is a gift given to you, and your job is to keep it precious every time you open it.

Juli Moody—professional athlete and stuntwoman

Matt DiRito
Courtesy of Dan DiRito Photography

Life is for learning. Humble yourself to the endless education that life provides, and learn to be a better person. The meaning of life is to become a bigger, better human being. To evolve— and that is a process, not a result. If you never arrive at the final destination, you've likely charted the perfect journey.

Don Wildman—Travel Channel TV host

CHAPTER TWO

IT'S THE RIDE, MAN!

I am personally one who says that kind of question is really irrelevant. It comes to mind that we are all here, and we must keep moving forward. Once we are comfortable with the unknown, we can ask that question. I have a keen interest in how we all got to this place at this moment, but that is born from the question, "How did we get here?," or more precisely, "Which came first, the chicken or the egg?" The answer is the egg. When we stop to wonder what the meaning of life is, we stop.

When I feel a little out of sorts as I am trying to go to sleep, I go out and look up at the sky. I have a very good understanding of the celestial sky. I am a celestial navigator. I look up and right now in the night sky I see the moon and Jupiter and Mars. The other objects are not important at this moment. I see our satellite (the moon) and two planets. I know I am in "the 'hood." I am in our solar system. I find balance in that knowledge. I feel grounded. The heavens are not frightful. In a way, they are duplicates of our galaxy. I am comfortable.

The question, as it is proposed in the frame of motorcycles, is much easier. The meaning of life is to get out and ride, which is moving forward. When one rides, one must focus. Riding motorcycles demands focus, and that focus is liberating. I truly enjoy riding alone. Long distances alone. No one else to determine the next moves. I stop when I want to stop. I stay where I want to stay. If it is raining before I start riding, I wait. If it starts raining while I am riding, I do not stop; I just ride a little slower and more carefully. I am moving forward through life. I will dry out while riding after it stops raining and I am still riding. In the state of fear one can't live like this, so learning to live without a shit pile of fear is quite challenging.

Peter Fonda—actor, writer, director, producer, activist, and philanthropist

Peter Fonda
Courtesy of Paul Field

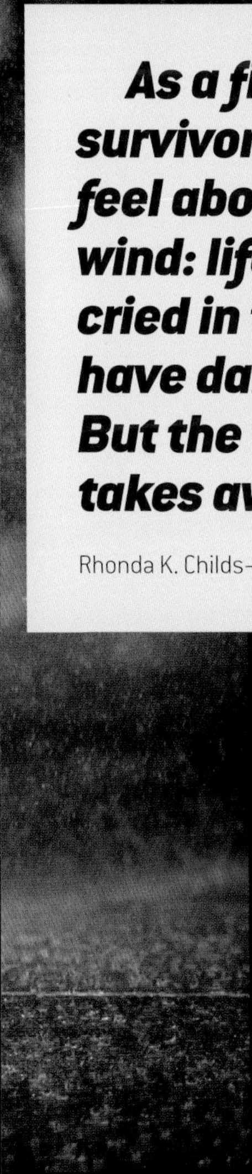

As a five-time cancer survivor, this is how I feel about riding the wind: life is hard. I have cried in the sunshine. I have danced in the rain. But the wind in my face takes away life's pain.

Rhonda K. Childs—retired LPN

Without my bike, life is just life.

Joe Battles—retired security

The freedom of the road, the beauty of the land, and the rush of the power between your legs is all undeniably a beautiful gift. Get out and ride!

Bryan Allen—owner of Southern Iron Kustoms

My meaning of life is living the "bike life"; it's the only life I want and the life I proudly choose to live. Being a biker isn't about the type of sled you ride, the clothes you wear, the tattoos you have, or anything else physical. Being a biker is having the love for the wind, respecting the Code, respecting each other, and involving yourself in charity and memorial rides. It's heartfelt.

It is about respect, loyalty, and honor. Any "Joe Blow" can play the part and make the look pass across ignorant eyes. A true biker rides with integrity and respect for the brotherhood of friends who become family, and the sense of freedom it brings. We ride for those in need with a heartfelt admiration for every cause we stand behind. Giving to and helping others is who we are and what we are about. We are loved and respected by our community for the good we do.

I am proud to be a biker, and when I can no longer ride, I pray there are sleds in heaven, for on the clouds I will cruise once again.

William "Gimp" Danford—heavy-equipment operator

Just ride. No worries that way. No rules. No one telling you what to do. Easy. I have been riding for thirty years and I love it, because it is true relaxation. Some people golf or bowl; I ride.

Jim Wingenbach—data center manager

I knew my meaning of life when I retired from daycare centers. I was under a lot of stress from working, so I got me a bike, and now I am just doing my own thing. I've always wanted to ride but just didn't have the time to do it before because I was raising five kids. Now I enjoy the freedom, the people, and riding in charity events.

Linda Titus—salesperson

Going to Sturgis. That's about all I do. I spend time getting ready for Sturgis, go home, and get ready for it again.

Jr. Sidwell—auto mechanic

To stay in the saddle as long as possible and to argue with my rabbi nonstop.

Scott Gottesman—electrician

Honesty, passion, and humility. The wind in your hair. And "don't play too-many notes!"

Sean McNabb—musician and actor

Sean McNabb
Courtesy of Jesse Silva

Courtesy of Paul Contreras, Beyond Photos Photography, Rio Rancho, NM

Being able to ride your motorcycle for two weeks across the country. Simple survival. I live by the code: "I am not a slave to a god that doesn't exist; I'm not a slave to a world that doesn't give a shit."—Marilyn Manson. Just as a safety precaution, I will repent on my deathbed.

Jason Sherrier—manager of packaging industry

It is what it is. I am what I am. You cannot have the good without the bad. One must be able to let go. Stumbling blocks are stepping stones. To be giving is how we receive. To teach is how we learn. One must be able to learn every day to become one with the all-knowing and the all-reality.

Kenny Olson—former lead guitarist with Kid Rock

Do things and live life to the fullest. That's how I explained it to my wife as to why I bought a Harley. I really enjoy riding my Harley because it gives me a sense of freedom. It gives me a chance to share great camaraderie with my friends, and it also gives me a chance to experience some of the most beautiful country in the US. Most people in my family are against me having a bike, but they understand and know that it is something that I feel very passionately about and really enjoy doing.

Alton Brown—publisher of *News & Advance*

Riding is my therapy. I don't have to text or talk with anyone else. I get to just be. When I am having a stressful time, I hit the road and let the wind, the sun, and the miles wash away my worries. Nothing else clears your mind and soul like the meditation of the motor and the road.

Scot Pollard—former NBA champion and *Survivor* TV series contestant

Waking in the morning knowing that I'm going for a ride. To no particular place. For no particular reason other than to enjoy the ride.

August Polito—senior national account manager

Ducati builds emotions. The world's most attractive motorcycles are the result of a deep commitment to racing competitions. They are the purest expression of refined skill, unmistakable design, and, above all, a great passion for bikes.

Ducati

Life is an opportunity, and it is what you make it. You can go through life stagnant, trying to make a dollar working for the man, or you can come here [Sturgis] and live life. Life is not about money; it's about whatever makes you happy. And right now, what makes me happy is riding with my posse, being on our bikes, riding free, and doing what we want, when we want. We had to bury a couple of our posse members in the last year, and that is why we're all so close. We love each other and tell each other every day.

"Beaner"—corrections officer

Motorcycles have always been the foundation of my life, from the first time I put my leg over one at age four until my first back flip on live national TV. As I get older and life transitions from athlete to businessman, to eventually family man, it will always be an important element of my life. My father and I bonded over motorcycles, and I look forward to one day doing the same with my child.

Even today, when Pink and I throw a leg over our Harleys to ride the coastline, it is the happiest place on earth for me. It is not just a pastime, a sport, or cool factor; it is a way of life for me. Actually, it is therapy.

When the day comes that I cannot ride my motorcycle anymore, just kick dirt over me and send me off, because I am not living if I cannot be on my motorcycle.

Carey Hart—retired freestyle motocross, motorcycle racer, off-road truck racer, and singer Pink's husband

Carey Hart
Courtesy of James Lissimore

When I think about the meaning of life, it all boils down to what my little brother always tells me: "We are not here for a long time; we are here for a good time! So why are we not partying now?"

Bob Parsons—founder of web hosting firm GoDaddy, entrepreneur, and philanthropist

It's getting a second chance. I thought about that lying in bed the night before my quadruple bypass, reflecting on my past and what got me there and the drive to live. I gave up smoking three packs a day at $5 a pack. After six years of putting away $15 a day, I applied it to the purchase of my bike. Also, now that my wife has been in remission from cancer for two years, I now enjoy this H.O.G. group and look forward to every ride, starting with the CHOC [Children's Hospital of Orange County] run.

Don Lavertue—service manager

Courtesy of Paul Contreras, Beyond Photos Photography, Rio Rancho, NM

Life is a gift, an opportunity, an encapsulation of the soul in a physical being. It is about making it better because you were here, whatever it is in any given situation. It is recognizing that we are not of this world and are just visiting for a period known as a life span.

The motorcycle is a gift that allows me to share His message on the road, spread goodwill wherever it allows me to go, and demonstrate that life is about faith, accountability, responsibility, and respect. Life is the embodiment of His love.

Christopher Parker—president of Faith Riders Motorcycle Ministry and corporate quality director

Motorcycling frees your soul. It begins when I shift into second out of my driveway, but it really makes sense when I hear, see, and smell the world from behind the handle bars. I am closer to what God created, managing the road on the back of my "Beemer." Oh, how it soothes the soul!

Howard Mudd—former NFL offensive line coach and offensive lineman

Sometimes it is best to not think, not obsess, simply breathe and take it all in. The world on a bike is full of wonder. It is all around; just open your eyes and mind and discover all that is around you. Every ride is an adventure and never the same for you or any rider.

Craig Berberich—entrepreneur

My life had such traumatic and dramatic changes—loss of a leg, loss of my career, loss of a house, loss of a husband, and loss of a family—and nothing made sense except writing. So writing really is my sounding board, the only place where I could even get any kind of quiet in my mind.

Riding is my narcotic, my antidepressant, and my sanctuary. In the saddle of my Harley, I learned how to live again, how to love again, and how to make peace with my higher power. So when death throws you back, ride.

Cat Hammes—registered nurse

Mitch Daniels
Courtesy of Mitch Daniels

Looking back after forty-five years and nine different motorcycles, the thing I love best is the growing variety of people who ride. The guy—or these days, the gal—on the next bike could come from anywhere and any walk of life. Today, there are far too few pursuits that bring folks together like that.

Mitch Daniels—president of Purdue University and former governor of Indiana

The meaning of life to me is simple. Mastery of one's life is like the mastery of a motorcycle: you learn to treat them both with respect. You keep up on the maintenance of relationships as well as your bike. When riding into the curves and over the hills, you learn to adjust to your surroundings, and you can always ride through the storms. As with life, the ups and downs, hard bumps, and curves life throws at you, you can overcome them all.

As with the start of a ride, as well as parking your bike at the end of the night, you know you have had a good day. Lay your head down each night with a clean conscience and know you have done the right thing. When you find peace within the ride of life, you have then found the meaning of life.

Jimmey Rodgers—semi tanker driver

I believe life is just an adventure-filled on-ramp for what is to come. It is designed to attack all of our senses with knowledge so we can be ready for the real game. Much like a child is taught to be kind by his or her parents, life is designed to teach us to accept and meet challenges, and to explore the myriad of reasons behind why we exist and what our purpose truly is. We have been blessed with the gift of reason for a reason. Life is just plain fun, even in its toughest times. If this is the beginning, I can't wait to see what is next.

Dr. George Marakas—owner of K and G Cycles and professor

Life is fun! Even though I have a university business degree, I have learned more about life while riding motorcycles than I could ever learn from a formal education. People will tell you that there are a dozen things money cannot buy: integrity, manners, morals, respect, character, common sense, trust, patience, class, happiness, love, and wisdom, but I disagree. While you cannot purchase these directly, you can buy a motorcycle, and if you ride it often and accumulate great distances solo or with others, you will learn each and every one of these traits. It is up to you how you implement them. Just remember, we have only two lives. The second one begins when we realize we have only one! And this brings me to the meaning of life: it is to live with all the aforementioned tenants while having fun and bringing some happiness into the lives of others.

Allan Roark—owner of Roark Torque

Riding is not a hobby; it is the meaning of life. It is the sights and smells, like rain on hot pavement. It is the people I have met all over the country. At a very young age I was a loner, and a motorcycle gave me peace and freedom. Going to some place that I have never been, being free, and having brothers in a club—this is life. Even after a very serious accident, I still got back on my bike.

Mark Eastman—electrician

Most of us spend a lifetime searching for the answer to the meaning of life. There are no right or wrong answers. It is how much of life you manage and how much you manage your life. Life happens more quickly as we age, and manages to slap us in the face from time to time. Hopefully lessons are learned, retained, and, more so, shared. You learn how to give of yourself, time, and help—have empathy and not judge.

Riding a motorcycle for fifty years makes you realize you've been in the movie the whole time, not just watching, especially when you ride to long-distance destinations, not just around town for a day. It is touching the road, the towns, and the wonderful characters we meet and befriend in those small towns along the way. You become a little part of each town and leave a little part of you in each town. No one understands the road trip until they take one on a bike.

Jeff Levy—retired mortgage banker

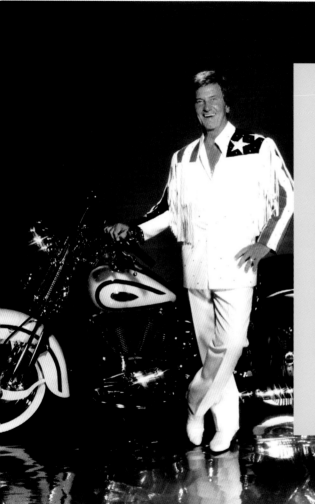

Believe it or not, I am a biker from way back. My wife and I had twin Suzuki big bikes years ago, until she took a nasty spill; she still bears the scars in her scalp and down her back as a reminder. Later, when I had a Harley Heritage Springer during my "Metal Mood" [No More Mr. Nice Guy recording days], I put a "sissy seat" on the back, expecting to take my grandkids for rides, but Grandma Shirley would never permit it (due to her unfortunate spill). I have never been a fan of riding on the freeway amidst the semis and speedsters, but riding a bike of any size on a country road on a sunny afternoon is heavenly. I even gave my dad his only motorcycle on his seventieth birthday, but that's another story.

Pat Boone—singer, actor, and author

Pat Boone
Courtesy of Pat Boone Enterprises

CHAPTER THREE

MAKE A DIFFERENCE

Health and happiness. My full meaning-of-life answer is tattooed on my shoulder—a Superman logo and underneath, in Latin, the words "While I Live, I Do Good." It is my moral compass. I have used this tattoo's message in a commencement address to our local high school, advising them to be more like Superman; not to leap tall buildings, etc., but to live for what the logo stands for: honesty, integrity, and doing good deeds for your family, community, and country.

Ron Gaffney—retired police officer

Find a passion and focus on a cause greater than yourself.

Gen. Richard B. Myers—US Air Force (Ret.),
four-star general; fifteenth chairman of the
Joint Chiefs of Staff; president of Kansas
State University

Gen. Richard B. Myers
Courtesy of Wikimedia Commons via DoD

Fulfilling dreams, making a difference, and having the time of my life while I'm on this earth. Growing up, I knew that I wanted to get married, have kids, and be a person my kids looked up to. My dreams fulfilled . . .

Having the opportunity to help kids at CHOC [Children's Hospital of Orange County], sponsoring a kid in Africa, and making time to share my life experience, I feel I am making a difference.

Jeff Chargualaf—sales manager

The meaning of my life has shown me how to give of myself, not just financially. I learned early on that I would be someone who would help many and never ask anything in return. I firmly believe if you leave out early, ride slower, you'll live longer. Be of service to your fellow brothers and sisters. Stand only as tall as the person you help and be a living example of what it truly means to be a biker.

Mike Garner—sign crewman for Franklin County
      Highway Department

Courtesy of ©Olivier de Vaulx / www.odvphoto.com

The meaning of life: changing and saving lives with Motorcycle Therapy. Providing this service and program to my fellow veteran brothers and sisters who have given and sacrificed so much to defend and preserve our way of life and this wonderful country brings purpose and meaning to my life. I have been riding motorcycles for forty-nine years, and I'll be providing Motorcycle Therapy to veterans until I can't ride anymore. So I figure I'm only halfway through.

Dave Frey—founder of Veterans Charity Ride

Live life helping others that are less fortunate than yourself, be the absolute best person you can, help put a smile on those that are going through a rough time, and lend an open ear and a shoulder to lean on. But most of all, love God and spread His word.

Be someone who inspires others, and do it because it is in your heart, not because you want something in return. I learned this from the Biker Nation, who does more for charity than anyone.

Paul "Torch" Resent—cancer fighter and advocate

Artie Muller
Courtesy of Lee Stalsworth

Doing what one can to help those in need without filling their pockets with money. All bikers give of themselves and their money.

Artie Muller—founder and executive director of Rolling Thunder Inc.

The meaning of life is kindness. To treat people the way you would like to be treated, to always be willing to give to those less fortunate and approach every situation thinking about the other person. Say hello, smile, and give a word of encouragement— simple acts that go a long way.

Kyle Petty—former NASCAR driver, current NBC Sports racing analyst, and founder of the Kyle Petty Charity Ride Across America

Kyle Petty
Courtesy of Kevin Kane Photography

Be kind to everyone and figure out what you were put on this earth to do. It has taken me fifty years to figure out why I am here and what it is that I am supposed to do with my life.

By creating a nonprofit organization, I am now at a stage where I can volunteer to help other veterans and their families in our area, especially during Thanksgiving and Christmas. And we also help veterans get a job. For example, if a guy has a job offer in Michigan but cannot afford to get there, we buy him a bus ticket and take him to the station. So right now that is my mission in life.

Dan Marvin—US Air Force (Ret.)

*Courtesy of Paul D'Andrea,
www.pdaphotography.com*

To make the world a better place to live than when I arrived.

Al Unser Jr.—two-time Indianapolis 500 winner and retired race car driver

The meaning of life is to serve. Serving others is one of life's most loving and sacrificial acts. Anyone can serve—young, old, rich, poor, or in between. Serving another person in need makes you vulnerable, and open to their hurt or burden. Looking the other way is the safe way through. I believe it is the vulnerability of motorcycles—being out in the world with all its threats and elements—that makes bikers so willing to help others. It is because we are out in the real world.

Terry Reilly—former executive director for Miracle Ride Foundation, Inc.

The meaning of life is to learn, grow, change, and help other human beings in the process. Everything we go through can—if we so choose—enable us to effect change within ourselves that can benefit and assist other fellow beings. As long as I live my life with that purpose, I feel fulfilled.

Billy Morrison—guitar player with Billy Idol and the Royal Machines, actor, and painter

Do one nice thing for one person every day.

Salvatore Dimisa—CAT scan technician

Making life better for others. It is as simple as that.

Duane "Digger" Carey—former NASA astronaut

The meaning of life is dependent on how one contributes to others and the reason we are put on Earth. Life is a state of mind, and what we do is based on how we feel about ourselves. The journey we are on may never be known to us but can be judged if we leave the world a better place to live. Life is about giving, sharing, teaching, and helping others to be the best they can be.

"Rocket Man"—realtor

Courtesy of Rev. Sal DiMisa

Duane "Digger" Carey
Courtesy of Duane "Digger" Carey

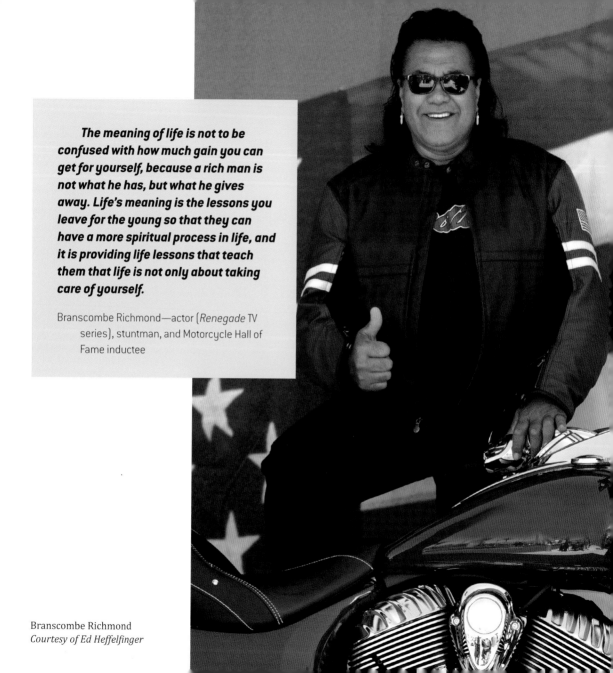

The meaning of life is not to be confused with how much gain you can get for yourself, because a rich man is not what he has, but what he gives away. Life's meaning is the lessons you leave for the young so that they can have a more spiritual process in life, and it is providing life lessons that teach them that life is not only about taking care of yourself.

Branscombe Richmond—actor (*Renegade* TV series), stuntman, and Motorcycle Hall of Fame inductee

Branscombe Richmond
Courtesy of Ed Heffelfinger

The answer changes from minute to minute. It is an accumulation of learning experiences. You learn and grow, or you repeat the same mistake over and over again. Our experience here is to have as much fun as possible and support as many charities as possible. The motorcycle enthusiast community is probably the bravest and most generous community out there. We just feel that it is all about helping as many people as possible.

Billy Gordon—executive director of Motorcycle Charity Associates

We have been blessed with the gift of life and all the possibilities it holds, and it is up to each of us to make the best of it. So what does that mean? I guess it is another way of saying, "What is the meaning of life?" Look out for your fellow man. Do the right thing. Step up and be counted. Don't succeed at the expense of others.

Rear Admiral H. E. "Rick" Grant—US Navy (Ret.)

It is the sacrifice of self so that another may live.

Wyclef Jean—rapper, musician, and actor

We were hurled into this world to try to justify or understand some reason why we are here. But of course we are driven by our basic needs, like food, friends, shelter, and so forth. Other than that, I guess it is about trying to help others when we are able to. That is what my life is about: doing what I need to do to have the bare essentials to be able to contribute to others—family, friends, and then to the rest of the world.

That is why I started the former Love Ride fundraiser ride in 1984. During its run, we raised over $25 million in funds for organizations such as the Muscular Dystrophy Association [MDA], United Service Organization [USO], Autism Speaks, and long-term support for the Glendale Community College. The 2015 Grand Finale's beneficiary was the Wounded Warrior Project. The Love Ride Foundation continues to help those in need, which is the true spirit and camaraderie that brought me to the motorcycle community in the first place.

Oliver Shokouh—owner of Harley-Davidson of
    Glendale and Sturgis Motorcycle Museum Hall of
    Fame inductee

***In the short time we
have here on Earth,
make a difference in the
lives of people in the
circle of our own life.***

Steve Alesio—former CEO and chairman of Dun &
    Bradstreet

***Do unto others as
you would have them
do unto you.***

Mike Holmgren—former president of the Cleveland
    Browns and NFL coach

The meaning of life is the way we conduct ourselves on life's journey, the decisions we make, and how we deal with the repercussions of those decisions. To live according to nature and not to fall into empty consumerism. To respect others and accept their differences without prejudice. To love and protect animals and the disadvantaged. And yes, to have some fun; make love, music, movies, and art. Enjoy life, a nice bike ride with friends, and sharing our passions and tastes.

Try to leave something honorable behind when we are gone so that we can say we did something positive in this life, and our presence on this earth was not like a parasite that just consumes and destroys. To love humanity and accept this imperfect world of ours. Always hope for its betterment.

Adolfo "Fito" de la Parra—drummer for Canned Heat

Being able to ride my bike for a worthwhile cause makes it that much more pleasurable. The auto-racing industry has a strong heritage of hosting benefit motorcycle rides, and I am proud to have participated in as many of them as my schedule allowed. A great example is Kyle Petty's Charity Ride, which has raised more than $18 million for the Victory Junction camp and other charities that support chronically ill children. That ride has logged more than 11.9 million cumulative miles, and it is a great opportunity for members of the NASCAR and GRAND-AM communities to kick back and enjoy themselves while helping a worthwhile cause.

James C. France—NASCAR vice chairman of the board of directors and executive vice president

Senator Kirk Watson
Courtesy of Daniel Davis

Use all you possess to serve others.

Senator Kirk Watson—Texas state senator

It is happiness in doing for others, and the journey.

Artimus Pyle—original drummer with Lynyrd Skynyrd and Rock and Roll Hall of Fame inductee

The meaning of life in this world is really all about what we make of our lives for the short time we are here. My parents taught me to give of myself, to help others as much as I could, and in return, life would take care of me and my family. The Army taught me to lead others at work and in life by my own example. My little secret throughout life has been to serve as a teacher, and to give the knowledge and wisdom I learned throughout life to those aspiring to climb the ladder behind me. Their success as individuals and the collective successes of each organization helped me find the meaning of my life. A satisfied life that afforded me the opportunity to do something meaningful and with purpose, to grow a family to love and serve future generations of this world, and the self-satisfaction of knowing I was able to help others achieve their dreams and goals. If today was my last day on Earth, and as I reflect back on my life from day one to present, acknowledging the mistakes I made and the subsequent lessons learned, I see what I have done to improve myself comprehensively, and I am happy and satisfied knowing I was able to teach and pass on these lessons of life.

Kenneth O. Preston—13th Sgt. Maj., US Army (Ret.)

To answer a question about the meaning of life, one must understand what life is. To me, life is always about choices. Choosing to act or not is in and of itself a choice. We can choose the path of greed and selfishness, or we can choose to make a difference. I chose to make a difference. Why? Because we all die. Why not make it count?

Richard McGuire—former mortgage broker and former aviator

What is the meaning of life is a question many are asked and wonder about daily. It is to look back on the past and have no regrets. Although we all have things that we would like to go back and change, I am talking about our interaction with others. Did we help others less fortunate when we could, or did we hinder them? Do we feel good about the memories others will have of us when we are gone? Will we bring a smile to someone's face when they think of us? There is not a single person who can be happy all the time, but there are those who are sad all the time. Sometimes the smallest gesture can bring a smile to show you care and believe: by riding in that charity run, donating, lifting a sick child up onto your motorcycle with their eyes wide, or seeing the relief on someone's face knowing they are not alone and have help with bills.

Mick Leonard—project manager

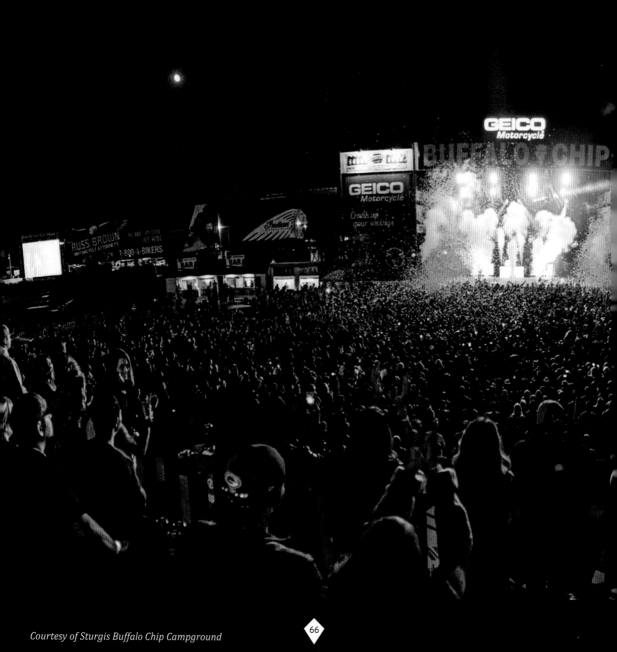

Courtesy of Sturgis Buffalo Chip Campground

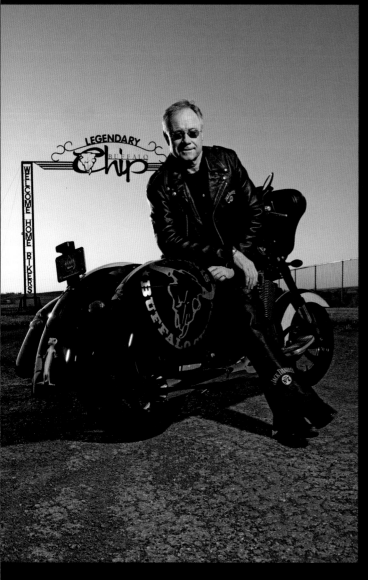

Rod Woodruff
Courtesy of Sturgis Buffalo Chip Campground

Personal fulfillment. Sit down and think what it is you want to get out of life in different areas—personal life, spiritual life, business life—and make a decision as to where you want to go. For each person there is a purpose in life, and it changes as you mature and get older.

The purpose of life should be to make the world around us a better place in our own little ways. To do that, we need to be able to reach out and touch the lives of other people. The more people you touch, the more impact you have.

Rod Woodruff—president and CEO of the Sturgis
Buffalo Chip Campground, Sturgis,
South Dakota

The meaning of life is like an investment account: the more you put into it, the greater the return. I believe this simple phrase can help guide any area of your life, from making crucial business decisions to raising your children. We each make our mark in this world by putting time and effort behind our talents, all in the pursuit of making a difference. The path of least resistance rarely leads to great rewards.

As a former law enforcement officer, I have a passion for motorcycles. I knew there had to be a way to put this passion to good use. I learned of an organization that helps survivors of fallen officers—C.O.P.S. [Concerns of Police Survivors]. I recalled from my days in law enforcement that an officer's biggest concern is not falling in the line of duty, but rather, what would happen to their family if they do. With that in mind, I decided to help this organization by starting Ride4COPS.

Harry Herington—chief executive officer and chairman of the board of NIC

The meaning of life for the Swords Brotherhood is that even though we all come from separate walks of life, we unite for a greater cause to help those in need, give our all to those who serve and protect us every day, and help the less fortunate and children with illnesses. United as one, we come together as a brotherhood to live life to the fullest and to help others live their lives to the fullest. Kindness makes life worth living.

Kenneth Barnes—certified kidney dialysis technician

Having lost my arm at fourteen years old, I thought that life was over for me. Life definitely changed from that moment. After much reflection on this event, I have come to the realization that this was just a hurdle that I needed to overcome, being that life is ever changing in an ebb-and-flow kind of way. Giving back is the way that we can all enjoy the feelings of life.

Jamie Eugene Pauls—mechanical designer

The meaning of life? I am still working on that and probably will till the end of my days, but I can tell you what I think it is not. It is not about grabbing all you can for yourself, and the rest be damned. It is not about being born a consumer and leaving nothing behind except your trash when you leave this earth. It is not about turning a blind eye to the need all around us, for we can all do something to lend a hand, no matter how little. The worst we can do is nothing.

John Kay—vocalist and front man for rock band
    Steppenwolf

John Kay
Courtesy of Daryl Bughman

Greater love hath no man than this, that a man lay down his life for his friends (John 15:13). It does not mean you have to die ... Although, having thirty-eight years as a career volunteer firefighter, I have seen many brothers die. It means do your absolute best to make a difference in someone else's life, daily. Simply hold a hand, lend an ear, open a door, buy a meal, mow your neighbor's yard, pay a utility bill, or organize a fundraiser. Look after the elderly, especially your parents. Pass on the opportunity to ridicule another person, and seize every teachable moment. In your time of need it will all come back to you.

John Hilfirty—firefighter and EMT

The meaning of life can mean many different things. As a hospice nurse, I see people take their last breath due to disease processes such as cancer, Parkinson's, chronic heart failure, etc. I know that life is precious and can be taken from us very easily, so I try to make my life as enjoyable as possible while God allows me to.

Life is also about making dreams and goals come true. Michigan Wind Sisters is a group of women who not only love to ride their own motorcycles but want to change how others perceive bikers. That is why we give back to the community by conducting events for local veterans, women's shelters, and children's groups, making sure a child does not go without food.

Leslie Yothers—hospice nurse and president and founder of Michigan Wind Sisters RC

Delegate Kathy Szeliga
Courtesy of Delegate Kathy Szeliga

To have a big heart like bikers do, no matter what size bike they ride! Wishing you warm weather, blue skies, and safe riding!

Delegate Kathy Szeliga—Maryland State Delegate and Minority Whip

CHAPTER FOUR

A HIGHER POWER

To follow God's will. And one of the best ways to figure that out is on the back of my 2003 Harley Davidson Road King, riding through the back roads of Wisconsin.

Governor Scott Walker—governor of Wisconsin

Governor Scott Walker
Courtesy of M. Scott Mahaskey / Politico

Enjoy life, while at the same time following God's beliefs from the Bible. We believe the Bible holds all the answers, and that as long as you follow that, you won't have too many problems.

Jabin and Stephanie White—construction; loan processor

To be inspirational to the life of everyone I meet. To be a good, godly person, and to let everybody know that there is a loving God who has restored my life, marriage, and health from drugs and alcohol. And from this time on, it is to experience everything possible on this planet with my loving wife.

Bill Young—general contractor

This life is only a stepping stone to eternity in Heaven.

Mickey Jones (1941–2018)—former drummer for Kenny Rogers and the First Edition, actor

Grow as a person and help others achieve, learn, and grow themselves. It is to eventually find meaning and purpose in this life. Realize that there is a greater Being and to find peace before you check out.

Ed Santiago—writer

Life is a gift from God to be lived to the fullest by centering it in the will of God. Having a real relationship with Jesus Christ enables me to ride my motorcycle with greater confidence.

Skip Heitzig—senior pastor of Calvary Albuquerque

I think we are put here with a purpose. The Lord has put something special in our hearts to follow. If we serve Him, we have a path and a duty to honor that and, one day, to return back to Him in Heaven. The only way to do that is through Jesus Christ.

Mike Hawkins—realtor and mortgage broker

Life is just a trial; a test to learn from the tough times, not knowing the reason for them. The meaning of life is to prepare for what comes next with God, which we also know little about.

Gary Tennison—human resources manager

It is all about how, in my short lifetime, I can be a representation of Jesus. I believe that God is our creator and His son Jesus is our savior. God created each one of us in His likeness and image, and it is our responsibility as humans to spread God's love among the peoples of the Earth. I got closer to God through motorcycling. Being exposed to the wonders of this great land while perched on the seat of my motorcycle provides me with the perfect lens with which to view the true nature of our Lord. I continue to experience the grace of God through my travels on a motorcycle.

Genevieve Schmitt—founder and editor of *Women Riders Now* online motorcycle magazine, and Sturgis Motorcycle Museum Hall of Fame inductee

Genevieve Schmitt
Courtesy of Genevieve Schmitt

Loving people. Sharing Christ. Transforming lives. The command of God implores, "Go into all the world and preach the gospel to all creation" (Mark 16:15). This is my life mission, and through the F.A.I.T.H. Riders Ministry, we/I take this calling seriously as the lifeblood of its existence and passion. The ministry—not a riding club or gang, and our/my sole purpose—is to share the life-changing Good News by equipping the saints to engage in practical ministry opportunities.

Dave Shride—senior product service coordinator and ministry director for Unity Baptist Church F.A.I.T.H. Riders

To understand the meaning of life, you must go back to its source, the Creator. As we grow in the knowledge of His Word, we begin to think and act as God does. Because God is love, it means that we will also learn to love our fellow man and minister God's healing love to all we meet. As we do this, God's Kingdom begins to be done on Earth as it is in Heaven.

Debby Haddon—retail sales

I believe God has a path, a reason we are all born. With that, it is the learning from our parents to be kind and merciful to our fellow animals of this earth, to honor our parents, and all those who teach and protect us. To meet each day with a new beginning of optimism to live that day to its fullest. Having faith that the life we live, the mate we find (our best friend), and the children we bear have a life of happiness and joy they deserve. To be able to see distress, anger, and sadness, and want to help those in need. To be there to share in all the good and reverence of family, friends, and mankind. To believe that when our time is done and God takes us, we have lived our life the best that we are able and to be at peace with death.

Chuck Vander Woude—truck driver

Find who and what God created us to be. I believe we are all born with gifts that God has given us. Some of us are lucky enough to discover these gifts and in some way act upon them. If we can incorporate them in our day-to-day life, it makes life much more interesting and rewarding.

William DeBilzan—artist

*Have a purpose and
to be true to the gifts
God gave you.*

Kenneth Sackowski—construction

I believe God created and placed us on this earth to serve Him through both living and giving. I do want to know that by the time that I am ready to die that I have lived my life fully to the best of my means and abilities. But life is not just about living, it is also about giving. I believe that you have not really lived life to the fullest until you have given back to someone else's life, to the people who cross your path. Therefore, the meaning of life to me is to give to someone so that I can experience life in its fullest measure.

Dean McKee—retail management

Having survived the '60s and Vietnam, and now accelerating through the baby boomer era, I am finding that the real meaning of life is coming from all that I learn after having thought I knew it all. I ride for the wind; it is what helps me focus on a higher power and not so much on myself. As life continues to pass by, I hope to only be more humble and kind.

Jim Loftis—retired equipment and truck operator

The meaning of life is about creating meaning. The universe has called us all here now to this world of impermanence for a reason, and that is to be uniquely ourselves and fulfill our higher calling. We are all beautifully different; therefore, what brings significance in our lives is different for each of us.

Meaning is not something we discover, nor that is taught. To the contrary, it is something we must create for ourselves to bring purpose into our lives and then apply that purpose to every situation, good or bad. This is done through living authentically, being in our truth, and cultivating our passions in any and all circumstances.

"For the vision of one man lends not its wings to another man. And even as each one of you stands alone in God's knowledge, so must each one of you be alone in his knowledge of God and in his understanding of the earth."—Kahlil Gibran

Jillian Michaels—leading fitness expert and world renowned life coach

Governor Mary Fallin
Courtesy of Jim Dillon, Dillon Foundation

The meaning of life is walking in faith to reach our individual potential and helping our fellow men, women, and children along the way.

Governor Mary Fallin—governor of Oklahoma

I have found out I have a terminal disease called idiopathic pulmonary fibrosis, which means my expiration is coming soon. This has given me the opportunity to get off the merry-go-round of my life and write, think, and talk to my end-of-life counselor. Throughout my life, I have been told that I am a strong woman, a survivor of much. The silver lining in all of this is a few years back my life needed sobriety to continue to live my life free from the monkey on my back, the damage occurring all around me. Through AA I did get sober, and, more than that, I developed a personal relationship with Jesus Christ that led me to a deep relationship with God and Jesus. My life didn't change overnight, but there were so many miracles, and some things changed faster than others. The meaning of life is to find the keys to the Kingdom, where I know there must be riding.

Brenda Mlodinoff—president of food company

Having lived sixty-plus years, I have come to believe that a truly fulfilled life is found in service to God. Through a relationship with Him, we find ourselves humbly serving others as directed by Him with the little time we are in this earthly realm. Service to others is where humans find not only happiness within themselves, but also peace with God and His other children.

Jeffrey Churchill—operations manager

To serve the Lord Jesus Christ with all my heart, mind, and soul, and to love my Brother as I would love myself. To help the needy and poor, to bring hope to those who have no hope, and to bring light into a world of darkness.

John Grice—director and founder of Bikers Against Hunger

To have a personal relationship with your Creator, one that gives you the purest thoughts, an honest living, abundance of joy, and unconditional love wherever your feet may roam.

Gina Cunningham—sales

I believe you find meaning in life when you discover what is more important to you than yourself. At an early age, it was all about me: my food, toys, and fun. As I grew up, I started recognizing that things were important. It was about accumulating stuff: cars, girls, motorcycles, and more and bigger toys. But when I got married, life took on a completely different aspect. Now I had to protect and love.

By this time, I was much less protective of me, and I wasn't very careful of life's potential for trouble. I was headed for disaster because I had no idea where I was going. I started looking outward and found others who were at peace with their lives. They all had one thing in common: they all knew a person named Jesus who had rescued them from a pit they had dug for themselves. I discovered that He was more important to me than me, and now my life is dedicated to Him. My meaning of life rests with Him. Where He sends me I will go.

Woodrow W. Weimer Jr.—retired business owner and retired military

Eddie Montgomery
Courtesy of Photography by Kristin Barlow

The meaning of life is pretty simple. If I have my family, music, friends, and God, I have everything I need. My life is so hectic from touring all over the country, and sometimes the world, that I like to keep things pretty simple at home. These things are what ground me and keep me going and doing what I love to do—entertain people.

Eddie Montgomery—country music artist, former member of country duo Montgomery Gentry

My philosophical outlook is this: Christ in you, the hope of glory. Christ through you, hope for the world. I want to be remembered as an obedient servant to the cause of Jesus Christ.

Rev. John R. "Zeke" Whitelock—founder and CEO of
      Alpha-Omegas Motorcycle Evangelistic Association

Here we are, in a universe bigger than we can imagine and more complex than we can understand. It is easy to feel small, even insignificant, but we are not. In each of us resides a spirit, and the spirit is here with purpose: to experience life. It wants to feel the warmth of the sun and share laughter with a friend. It will find passion and love, and it will endure pain and loss. Life will bring with it the good and the bad. There will be mountains and valleys. This is the adventure. This is the ride. The meaning, the purpose, is to live life and live it well. We are here to experience each day, filling our spirits with "this thing called life" and enjoying the ride. Fearlessly.

Debbie Pearl—board member of Rock and Ride for
      the Cure

As we ponder through life's struggles, we often look to God to fix our problems, but it seems we want him to do so on our terms and in our time. We get so caught up in the way we think things should be done that we often overlook the grace He may be bestowing on us right in front of our eyes. Sometimes answered prayers come in ways that we tend to overlook.

Kelly Joiner—acquisition analyst

As a pastor of faith, God gives me meaning. As a musician, I find meaning in sharing the talents God gave me. As a biker, meaning comes from twisties and an open road. So when I put everything together, I come up with sharing my faith through music and life and taking a little time to enjoy the ride.

Doug Briney—musician and pastor

CHAPTER FIVE

THE OTHER "F" WORDS

Good clean fun.

Gregg Allman (1947–2017)—rock and blues
  singer-songwriter, keyboardist, guitarist, and a
  founding member with brother Duane of the
  Allman Brothers Band

Life is to be treasured. Life means the sum total of your accomplishments in this life . . . what we leave in our footsteps when we depart the real world. Life is family and all about family: La Famiglia Primo, the family first. Your children should be shown the graciousness of your existence and the things you did that show your character, especially when no one is looking. It is what is in our hearts and how we express our gratitude toward others that speaks volumes for who we are. Life is your material accomplishment, too. Making a good living by serving others and making their lives better through you touching them in some way.

Ron Catronio—sales trainer, writer, motivational speaker,
  and cofounder of Big Bike Riders Children's Foundation

Gregg Allman
Courtesy of Danny Clinch

Being free from a lot of things—drugs and alcohol would be one.

Rudy Sanchez—auto mechanic

While I believe the meaning of life can be a complex question, it is truly in the eye of the beholder. For me, I'd boil it down to a few things. First, I think we should all endeavor to leave the woodpile a little bit higher than we find it, in whatever we do, personally or professionally.

Professionally speaking, Teddy Roosevelt once said: "Far and away the best prize that life has to offer is the chance to work hard at work worth doing." And as a certified workaholic that certainly has resonated with me, and I am very blessed to have done that in numerous jobs over the years. I would also add that working with people you respect and enjoy working with is also important.

Lastly, and certainly not the least, life is about relationships with your God, your family, your friends, and your colleagues. To all these I also consider myself extraordinarily blessed.

Winston Kelley—executive director of NASCAR Hall of Fame, announcer with Motor Racing Network

Living out your dreams with no regrets. Taking a job for the love of it, not the money. People come and go in your life, but family is forever.

Jay LaRossa—owner and CEO of Lossa Engineering

I thought I was living for the first forty years of my life, but I was wrong. I started living on December 4, 1999, when my daughter Chyna was born. The meaning of life for me is my beautiful little girl, because without her, life is meaningless.

Steve Kolstad—purchasing manager

Courtesy of Steve Smith

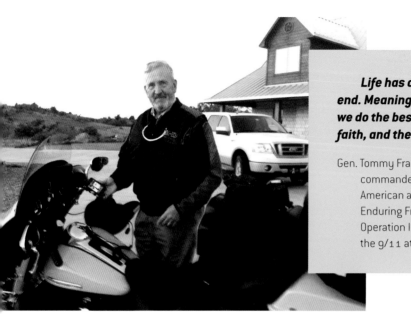

Life has a beginning, a middle, and an end. Meaning is found in the middle, where we do the best we can by our families, our faith, and the American flag.

Gen. Tommy Franks—US Army (Ret.), former commander in chief, US Central Command. Led American and Coalition troops in Operation Enduring Freedom in Afghanistan and Operation Iraqi Freedom in Iraq in response to the 9/11 attacks

The meaning of life has had many meanings at many different times. It is experiencing and digesting every moment and looking for the gifts from each one. You have to be open to them; otherwise you miss them— the birth of your child, riding through our country and seeing its beauty, enjoying family and friends, and bringing joy to others. It is about blessings—giving them and receiving them, and choosing to see them or not.

In loss there is positive as well, if you are open to it. My heart was broken when I lost my youngest sister to breast cancer. But the love and support from my riding friends has been amazing and allowed me to create an event that is now in its seventh year in raising money for Harley's Angels Cruzin' To Cure in the fight against breast cancer.

Bob Newlin—aircraft mechanic for NASA contractor

To live free. Living free means to make my own decisions about how I want to live my life, where I want to go, and what I want to do. Being in the military, you have to make certain sacrifices, but it is worth it to make sure everyone else is free. I never knew what freedom meant until I was in the military for about ten years. It was at that time that I got married, started a family, and made the decision to make the military a career. That is when freedom became a part of me, knowing that my family's freedom was as important, if not more so, than my own.

Shawn Holmes—Florida Air National Guard, homeland defense

The world has become cluttered with rules, regulations, and silly legislation concocted by out-of-touch bureaucrats. As a result, one's sense of freedom—the feeling of being free to live an authentic life based on personal choices and aspirations— is significantly compromised, if not impossible, for most people today. This is one of the main reasons why I love motorcycling. Riding allows me to find a sense of freedom away from this bureaucratic encroachment and overreach.

Yes, I am chasing freedom, so every ride matters and every mile counts toward this end.

Marc J. Beaulieu—president and CEO Motorcycle Marc Media

Live your life worthy of those who sacrificed their lives for our freedom. Live free and let your spirit fly. Make them proud.

Bill Geary—construction general superintendent

I thought happiness was when I opened my own restaurant on the thirty-fourth floor of a building. I had lots of friends, and I thought that was success. But the friends I had were, as my mom calls them, fair-weather friends. As long as I had a large wad of cash in my pocket, I had a large entourage. After I closed my restaurant to take care of my mom after her strokes, I was left with five key friends who were there to support me. And whenever I am down, they are always there to give me that strong pep talk. That is true success right there.

Marcos Rojas—retired restaurateur and caregiver

Family, friends, and a seventy-mile-an-hour wind in my face while on my Softtail Deluxe. Enjoy every day and ride like it's your last.

Bo Bice—singer, musician, and *American Idol* runner-up

Bo Bice
Courtesy of Love Imagery

For me, riding is fun because I can get a sense of freedom, feel the fresh air, and get a greater view of the planet and the beauty around us. Whereas if you're in a cage—what we call a car or truck—you have a singular vision out the front windshield and you miss the whole world all around you. You'd be amazed at what you see and hear on a bike when you have 180-degree vision. It is an amazing feeling. That's why we call it "wind therapy."

Todd Talbot—imagery intelligence analyst

To be free and live so that you have enough. Enough love, sense, money, compassion, faith, character, and personality. Not over the top; just have enough to be happy and live for your brother.

Wendell and MaryAnn Peters—operations coordinator; retired educator

The meaning of life has to do with being there, in all ways, for those who are living with you during this lifetime. Family, friends, yes, but also absolutely beyond to all who share life's needs with which you should enjoy assisting through care, kindness, and universal love.

Dr. Martin J. Rosenblum (1946–2014)—historian emeritus for Harley-Davidson, poet, and musician

Waking up each morning and thanking God for giving me another day to be everything I have always wanted to be—a biker. From age twelve I have been riding motorcycles, and each day from that point in my life I have learned the true meaning of family. The true meanings of love, loyalty, honor, and respect have been in my life for a very long time. There are very few things in my life that I would change, but I can assure anyone that the part of being in the biker family is my true meaning of life.

Ronnie Johnson—retired from chemical disposal industry

Courtesy of Steven Scaffidi, Ghost Rider Pictures

Vanilla Ice
Courtesy of Isaiah Trickey

The meaning of life is family and friends. Nothing else in life compares. It is just that simple. Give anyone all the money or material things they ever wanted and sit them in the middle of the desert, and I guarantee you they would trade it all to be with their family and friends. So the meaning of life is to enjoy life. There is no greater joy.

Vanilla Ice—rapper, actor, and host of DIY Network's *The Vanilla Ice Project*

Family, faith, and friends—the three legs of the life stool. Without three, the stool tumbles. Regardless of your age, race, color, religion, or physical attributes, it is faith, family, and friends that are what are really important in life. Add God's word on helping others, and the journey becomes filled with love, wonderment, excitement, thrill, joy, challenge, laughter, and fulfillment. The journey, helping others, and family, faith, and friends make for the true meaning of life.

John Eller—business value consultant

My son's blue eyes. In his eyes I see the past, the present, and future. I see pureness of soul, honesty, and love.

Gary Spellman—cofounder of Ultimate Face
        Cosmetics, cofounder of the Peace Love
        Happiness Charity Motorcycle Ride, and Sturgis
        Hall of Fame inductee

Some say the meaning of life is to reproduce, raise your young to be responsible and caring individuals who can on their own contribute to society, and continue the cycle of life. Each day I am happy to be alive, and each night I think it could be my last, mostly due to my health issues. So as the story goes: Each day live, love, laugh, and be happy.

Glenn Dickey—product development engineer

Not to be forgotten, but to be remembered after you are gone. I do not necessarily believe in life after death, but I believe that you never die if people remember you. I think my family and friends will remember me well, but eventually they will forget. I just want them to remember me with love, because I certainly don't want them remembering me as an asshole!

Clarence Wheeler—US Army (Ret.)

Forgive those who can't keep up in life, as we hope all others will forgive us when we can't keep up.

Perry King—TV and film actor, and AMA Motorcycle
        Hall of Fame inductee

Perry King
Courtesy of Jesse Leake

> *You never outgrow freedom: freedom on the road, freedom to choose your life, and the fight for freedom here in Washington, DC.*

Congressman Darrell Issa—US House of Representatives for California's 49th Congressional District

---

I lost my dad from a sudden heart attack. Extensive damage called for the decision to disconnect him from life support. I was the one to make the decision, and it is something I have to live with on a daily basis. Soon after my dad died, I had a tattoo put on my back of the sun's rays coming through some clouds. On the first three mornings of this road trip, the sky displayed sun rays coming through the clouds, exactly like my tattoo. It was very reassuring to know my dad was with us, keeping us safe.

Chris Colby—telecommunications

I lost a really good friend and mentor, James. It came natural to James to just give, never taking credit; he got more satisfaction out of helping others. One morning, fifty-five-year-old James went about his normal routine, kissed his wife as he left for work, and without warning dropped dead at her feet. At the funeral, I learned from James's wife that he considered me his best friend, too.

I look around and see that so many people are in it just for themselves, but it is really about giving. Everybody wants to be "badass." Whatever happened to just being the "good guy"? Let's just have the courage to be good, like my friend James.

Mike "Kiwi" Tomas—owner of Kiwi Indian Motorcycles

The meaning of life has something to do with meaningful connections with others, learning from our experiences, and how engaging in both moves us all forward. The connections could be about positive things like love, friendship, and mentorship, or about connections and experiences that we perceive as negative. Trusting that the universal consciousness has a plan and that our part in it is to engage with others and learn from our experiences is key, not just for understanding the whys and whats, but also for acceptance and happiness. In response to those who question their existence with the inevitable "Why bother?," I reply with my favorite Gandhi quote: "Whatever you do in life will be insignificant, but it is very important that you do it."

Deme Spy—Biker Entourage, managing member

Charlie Brechtel
Courtesy of Cameron Carbrey

The freedom of what we do. Lots of folks who are working at their jobs and typing away look out their windows and see me riding, and they would love to be me. Being on the open road and being free. That is what our country is built on.

Charlie Brechtel—founder and co-owner of Bikers Inner Circle Radio and founding member of the Charlie Brechtel Band

The meaning of life is being with all of my military brothers and serving others. Once you get out of the military, you are always still in the military. I still think I can jump off bridges and dive the deepest depths. Of course I can't because I'm old, but these guys— my military brothers—help me remember.

Ray Straining—US Navy diver (Ret.) and computer engineer

My meaning of life is family. Because of the amount of time I spent away from family, I found how much they were a part of my life. The times I spent away on cruise with the Navy for six months at a time (all eight times) has given me that focused insight. As I grow older, I have found that my four daughters are the apples of my eye.

Now I have other family members, and also my brothers and sister from my motorcycle riding group, the Combat Veterans Motorcycle Association (CVMA), here in North Carolina. Most of them are former Army or still active, but they have accepted me and my wife with open arms even though I am retired Navy. We raise money for veterans in need and volunteer to help those who need help. Hands down, without family, there would be no life worth living.

Martin Nielsen—chief warrant officer (CWO4), US Navy (Ret.)

God, family, and friends. I thank God for the life He has given me. I thank my parents for the upbringing they gave me. I am grateful for all the family that is and has been in my life. And I am thankful for all my friends with whom I have been surrounded through my journey of life. But most of all, I am thankful for all the love that I have been blessed with, because love is the greatest gift of all. I may not have much money, but I am richly blessed with the best family and friends any guy could ever have.

Danny C. Lolley—truck driver

As a biker girl, it is the brothers and sisters we meet through our rides and the functions we do in the community. It is a special lifestyle, and only bikers understand. We all have lost people in our lives. I lost my husband and fifteen-year-old son, but family was there for me, as well as my biker family. What regular people don't get is that once you have bikers in your life, that family is the glue that holds it all together.

Cathy Lydem—school bus driver

Life, as we have come to understand, is an experience, and when we are observant of its details, we ultimately learn and grow. As I have encountered through this revealing and enlightening process, it is also an exhilarating thrill ride living in faith every day.

Life's bumpy ride has taught me that it is best to have faith in something far bigger than oneself to roll down life's ever-alluring black-ribbon highways of self-discovery. Faith helps one become aware of all of life's unsuspecting bumps and dings. It helps to keep your shiny side up when forced to power through all those treacherous twists and turns, and lets you hold on tight while twisting the throttle rolling through the ups, and then over, to softly braking while enduring the downs.

Kevin "James" Richardson—retired general building contractor, writer, and spiritual vagabond

Courtesy of Ed Richtsteig

Gilby Clarke
Courtesy of Kathy Flynn

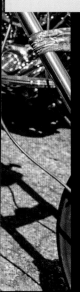

I always thought it was about connection, but after so many years of traveling and living like a gypsy, I am losing faith in mankind. Now the meaning of life, for me, is the pursuit of freedom—freedom of thought, expression, and, of course, Being. Without it, I do not think you can truly experience anything internally or externally, or participate in any truth that exists.

Gilby Clarke—guitarist, songwriter, record producer, and former guitarist with Guns N' Roses

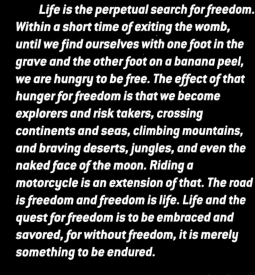

Life is the perpetual search for freedom. Within a short time of exiting the womb, until we find ourselves with one foot in the grave and the other foot on a banana peel, we are hungry to be free. The effect of that hunger for freedom is that we become explorers and risk takers, crossing continents and seas, climbing mountains, and braving deserts, jungles, and even the naked face of the moon. Riding a motorcycle is an extension of that. The road is freedom and freedom is life. Life and the quest for freedom is to be embraced and savored, for without freedom, it is merely something to be endured.

James Groh—operations specialist, US Navy (Ret.), and executive producer of *2 Old Goats on Hogs* TV show

CHAPTER SIX

WHO KNOWS?

Robert Patrick
Courtesy of Hillsides

I have no idea.

Robert Patrick—film and TV actor (*Terminator 2: Judgment Day*, *Scorpion*, *The X-Files*)

The good Lord puts each of us on Earth for a purpose. The meaning of life is to uncover our unique purpose and fulfill it. Discerning that purpose, for many of us, is a lifelong pursuit. You're never really sure.
Riding a motorcycle is a great way of addressing this challenge. The heightened awareness of danger, combined with a lack of other distractions, can really focus the mind.

James C. Miller III—served as chairman of the Federal Trade Commission and as budget director for President Ronald Reagan

Danny Bonaduce
Courtesy of Danny Bonaduce

I don't know the meaning of life, and even if I did, who is to say that the meaning of my life has any bearing on the meaning of your life. But I can tell you what makes life worth living: chicks.

Danny Bonaduce—former child actor (*The Partridge Family*) and radio personality

Courtesy of Behind Barz *Motorcycle Magazine*

Good question. I have pondered this in the past. Why are we here? Why are we the only self-aware beings on the planet? Are we the product of evolution, or did God design evolution that somehow resulted in the Garden of Eden?

I think as self-aware beings we should be kind to other people and beings. I use common sense to strive to enjoy life without impacting others in a negative way and to enjoy family and friends.

When I "check out," I believe it is at that moment I will be truly aware of what the meaning of life is, because nobody really knows.

Steve Melton—retired

As far as the meaning of life, I'm still searching. However, I do have a few ideas on what gives life meaning: (1) Always have something to look forward to. It could be something big, like a long out-of-state ride that will cover a week or more, or something small, like meeting a friend for a pint on Tuesday. (2) The most-important liquids of life are blood, beer, coffee, and whiskey. (3) There is nothing better than a good cheeseburger. (4) Travel. Get outside your comfort zone and see the world. (5) The best conversations are had around a campfire. (6) Challenge yourself. We get old only when we decide we have nothing left we can learn. (7) Read, constantly. The second you finish one book, start another. (8) All things in moderation, especially politics. (9) Hard work is its own reward. (10) Enjoy every sandwich.

Geoff Hughes—nurse practitioner

> **Heck if I know. I am just trying it out day by day, taking it one day at a time.**
>
> Richard Rutledge—self-employed

If I knew the answer to this question I wouldn't be here; I'd be a millionaire. With that said, I believe we are all put here with a purpose. If one is lucky enough to find his or her purpose in life, that is as close as we can come to finding the meaning of life.

David Love—attorney

I do not know the meaning yet, but I believe family is very important. Not that I was trying to, but somehow I put off having one, as I have never been married and don't have children. And yet the older I get, the more I think that family is what is important.

I still have meaning in my life because I have an effect on other people in a positive way by who I am—compassionate and understanding. I have met many people who have needed that at certain times in their lives, and I think I have helped people. So I guess I do feel that the meaning of life

It is amazing that we are even able to contemplate that question. There are endless ways to interpret it. Ironically, we don't really know the answer and will spend our lives looking for it. Even more ironically, its meaning can change for us as we move through our personal experiences and challenges.

It is an elusive mind fuck, so why bother? What's so wrong with not knowing the answer anyway? We should ask rather why it makes us so uncomfortable not to know. That's really the only part of this riddle that you can put a nail to.

In the meantime, make as much love, take as much love, and share as much love as you can. Embrace your every day, be nice, and play well with others.

Timothy White—famed celebrity photographer

Timothy White
Courtesy of Travis Shinn

At forty-four years old, I am still trying to figure it out. I could sit here for an hour or a few days and still not come up with anything. Just figuring it out.

Mark Rutan—courier messenger

The real meaning of life? No one knows, so grab it by the handle bars and ride it to wherever it takes you.

Carlos Mencia—comedian, writer, and actor

You got me!

Terry Holmes—retired

I don't know. The meaning of life is something that I learn as I grow. It is the love that you give to your husband and your children; there is nothing stronger in life than that bond you have with your children. As my children grow into adults, I see so much of my husband and me in them. I look back at so many things that I wish I could have done differently, but I am proud of my children and that is a very strong meaning of life.

Dana Theobald—pharmacy technician

The meaning of life has become lost. We no longer live, we exist. Life should mean being happy. Being adventurous. Being respectful. Being grateful and appreciative for who and what we have in our lives. Hard working, yet hard playing.

Chant Owen—network technician electronic

Tom Berenger
Courtesy of Tom Berenger

What is the meaning of life? It is one of the most prolific questions of mankind, whether spoken aloud or simply thought. I actually did ask a priest acquaintance this very question many years ago. He cocked an eye, shot me a half smile, and replied, "No one knows. It's a mystery."

So maybe that's it, or perhaps a combination of hospitality, responsibility, generosity, sympathy, forgiveness, and love. Yeah, maybe that's it.

Tom Berenger—Oscar nominee and Golden Globe—
and Emmy-winning actor

Bacon. Yep, definitely BACON.

Chuck Bullock—semiretired contractor

CHAPTER SEVEN

CHAPS SLAPPIN' HAPPY

Be as happy as I possibly can. To learn from life experiences and lessons so that others and I can be happy and make the world a better place to live by supporting and helping humanity and the environment because we are here.

John Paul DeJoria—founder of Patrón Spirits, John Paul Mitchell Systems, and John Paul Pet

Well, that's a good question. If I were in a beauty pageant, I probably would have a real long answer. But being that I am not, my life is just day to day. Every day that I can get up and put my feet on the ground, I'm feeling pretty good.

Dan Whittier—director of court services

John Paul DeJoria
*Courtesy of John Paul and his Top Fuel
champion daughter, Alexis DeJoria*

Courtesy of Sandi Long, photographer for
POW*MIA Awareness Rally, Pocatello, ID

I don't think you find out the meaning of life until you turn forty, because I didn't find it out until I turned forty. It's all about making me happy. Everything I want to do, I do it. Don't worry about money. Don't worry about nothing. Just taking risks and enjoying it day by day.

Beverly Drope—business owner

We at BMW Motorrad support our riders every day by providing them with the highest-quality products to make their ride an enjoyable one, whether traveling the world or sporty riding on winding roads. Knowing that our loyal customers are happy riding our motorcycles all over the world gives BMW Motorrad purpose and meaning in our work.

BMW Motorrad

Love is the meaning of life and gives all meaning to life. To love is the best gift you can give, and to be loved is the best gift you can receive. Nothing else compares. Be awesome.

Jay Blanchard—software engineer

Courtesy of Ed Richtsteig

The meaning of life is making it to tomorrow with a few laughs on the way.

Richard Kind—stage, film, and TV actor (*Spin City*, *Mad About You*)

I believe the adage "the pursuit of happiness" is the meaning of life. That probably sounds selfish, and I suppose it is a bit. But happiness is also very selfless. Giving to others and caring for others can make one very happy. It always amazes me how many people will sacrifice their happiness for things that do not warrant a passing thought. Life is just not worth living if it is spent in misery.

Funny how many wealthy people are so miserable, so it is not about money. It is about making the effort to look at your life honestly and then having the courage to do what it takes to be happy: changing jobs, moving, getting married, or getting divorced can all be challenging things to do, and many times require courage. Yet so many settle for mediocrity and sacrifice their happiness out of fear or other emotions that just distract you from being happy.

Steve Mortell—supervisor

The meaning of life is to just be the best person I can so that I can look back with no regrets. Be kind whenever I can and leave things as good or better than I found them. Make my puppy feel like the king of the world, and ride whenever I can without getting run over, of course.

Steve McCammon—actor

Wow, that's a tough one! No one has ever asked me that in a courtroom before. If these guys weren't standing around me right now, I would say that love is the meaning of life. Peace, love, and understanding are the meaning of life.

Hayes Young—lawyer

Pursuing things that make you happy and doing whatever you want to do. And be respectful of others that surround you.

Humberto Muraro—truck driver

Make everybody happy. Be happy with yourself, share that happiness, and make life better for everyone.

Frank Jewell—jewelry designer

Follow your dreams and your passions. Being true to yourself and being good to people. And eating well.

Cathy Coster—executive assistant

Norman Reedus
Courtesy of Adam Ewing

Finding happiness.

Norman Reedus—actor (*Walking Dead* TV series)

To find joy. Kids are really good at it. Watch one for five minutes, and you will see the telltale signs: a raised eyebrow, a wide-eyed expression, a little shriek. As we get older, we somehow lose touch with the wonder of life. With six kids, I get to witness joy all the time.

Lorenzo Lamas—former film and TV actor (*Renegade,*
Bold and the Beautiful, Grease)

Lorenzo Lamas
Courtesy of the Boot Campaign
(www.bootcampaign.org)

The meaning of life is getting out in the country, having a good time, and trying to be a good person.

Salvatore Arcabascio—fire department mechanic

Having what you want but, more importantly, wanting what you have.

Kimberly Love—GI technician

Man is, that he might have joy. Of all the things I have collected in life, the old souls I have gathered mean the most. Motorcycling is only the common thread that brings my art to others and them to me.

Jeff Decker—sculptor licensed by Harley-Davidson

Just to enjoy friends and family, and to get out and enjoy things. So when your time comes, you don't look back on it and say, "I wish I had . . ." or "I wish I did . . ." You can say, "I did it." Just enjoying everything the most you can.

Jeff Stubblefield—licensed practical nurse

The meaning of life is the pursuit of joy and contentment. Joy and contentment are often felt as the fluid in your inner ear accelerates past the sensitive follicles therein. This is most easily attained by twisting the right grip on your favorite motorcycle.

Kawasaki Motors Corp., USA

Life is meant to be lived to the fullest. To be happy with what you have and to treasure God's gifts.

Fabio—model, spokesman, and actor

Fabio
Courtesy of Fabio, Inc.

The meaning of life is to be content in all circumstances. I am currently attending a church called the Big House Inc. in Tempe, Arizona. We are a church made up mostly of bikers, and it is so cool to be able to ride to church, wear your riding clothes, and be accepted by everyone for who you are. I don't feel the need to put up a front for anyone; just worship God and enjoy the fellowship of others who are like minded.

My two sons are twenty-three and eighteen—they both ride Harleys—and it is so cool to go for a ride with both of them and share our passion for motorcycling. I am glad they embraced the lifestyle. I used to take them on rides in my side car, and now I am riding alongside them.

Ted Barrett—Major League Baseball World Series umpire and crew chief

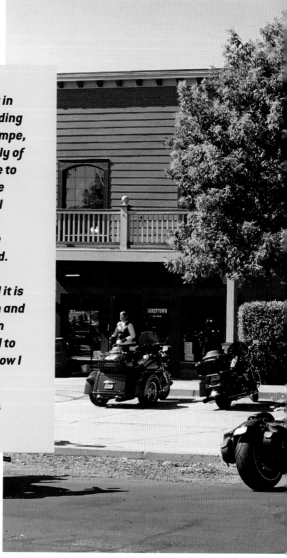

Courtesy of Jamestown Harley-Davidson

There is no bigger happiness than to help others and make other people happy. There are no strangers, only friends you haven't met yet.

Arne Bakke—locksmith

To be respectful, caring, and loving.

Richard Aquilia—postal worker

To find the feeling of love in its pure form. To allow this to hold your heart and flow this infinite love to all those around you. To love, serve, and remember love.

Scott Ryals—motorcycle parts

The meaning of life is the opportunity to take as many risks as you can, and hopefully find happiness in doing so. Without taking risks and chasing dreams, we fall into the same doldrums of everyday routines, which in my opinion is just existing. It means getting through this life with integrity and a purpose and living every day with happiness in your heart and soul.

Missy Covill—retired welder and musician in the band Iron Cowgirl Missy

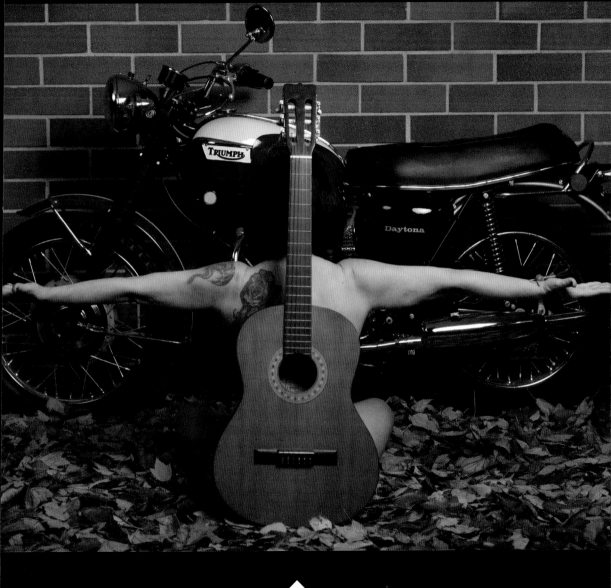

Courtesy of Assunta + Russell Photographers

CHAPTER EIGHT

THROTTLE THROUGH WITH GUSTO

We are here to help others and spread as much joy and love as we can while we are on this earth. Life is meant to be lived, not wasted or taken for granted. Each day is truly a gift, so do things that you love and find your passion. I tell my kids to find what you love to do and do it. (And if you can make a living at it, then that's even more wonderful!) Find a job you love. I don't care if it is picking up garbage; just do it well and with as much love in your heart as you can find. Do what you love and don't be afraid of what people think of you. Take chances and challenge yourself, for that is where the biggest growth comes from. Smile at strangers and always be kind. Most of all, remember that it is not the years in your life, it's the life in your years.

Cris Sommer-Simmons—author, AMA Motorcycle Hall of Fame inductee, Sturgis Motorcycle Museum Hall of Fame inductee, National Motorcycle Museum Hall of Fame inductee, three-time Motorcycle Cannonball finisher, and Women's editor for *American Iron Magazine*

Cris Sommer-Simmons
Courtesy of Cris Sommer-Simmons

> **Live wide open without regret. Full throttle until you see God, then brake.**

Scott Adams—truck driver

My life-changing experience came on February 10, 1996—the day I stopped drinking. (Until that day, my life had been on a slow, downward spiral that I could not see or didn't want to see.) I went to the hospital that day with what turned out to be pancreatitis caused directly from a long period of daily drinking, from age thirteen to forty-five. According to the doctors, I was nearing death's door.

I recovered and started a journey of rediscovery of myself and of a sober life. On this journey I found a God of my understanding and a dedication to live a better life one day at a time. Everything I have today is due to this life-changing day—my business, parents, children, and fiancé, and her children, would not be part of my life.

My journey teaches me that I am not a bad person, but I was a very sick individual who did bad things while drinking. Being sober has allowed me to be who God wants me to be each and every day that I wake up and take a breath of air. I also know that I am not perfect and do not always do the right thing every time, but today I can correct my mistakes because I have the courage to face them head on and not alone, but with my God, instead of hiding behind a bottle.

Matt Beischlag—tool-and-die industry

Over the years and time, I am sure my response and answers to "What is the meaning of life?" have changed many times. I feel that you need to do things correctly, for a lifetime is fleeting. If you are going to do something, do it right. Aim big, be big. Aim small, be small. Enjoy what you can, be trustworthy and true, and try to be yourself. As I said, life is fleeting. There will be regrets; there will be rewards. Believe and hold family and friends in high regard. You are here for a reason. Make the most of it. I hope that by caring in some way, my life had meaning.

Wally Elliott—marketing manager, manufacturers' rep, and DuKane ABATE events coordinator

The meaning of life is to do your best with what you have been given. Be honest and fair with others. Make good choices and stand by your choices. Love and be true to your country.

Kim Stoldt—school teacher

It's a day at a time. Live for now.

Paul Johnson—owner of Pig Trail Harley-Davidson

Quality of life. I have seen a lot of cancer, a lot of sadness in my life, a lot of dying, and I believe the meaning of life is quality of life. After you raise your children and do a good job, you should enjoy your life any way you can.

Ineta Kohler—homemaker

Faster horses. Older whiskey. Younger women. More money.

Tom Mondo—company pilot for the movie industry

Ian Anderson
Courtesy of Nick Harrison for Ian Anderson

Either (a) Darwinian survival, blessed and cursed with mysterious soul, (b) the fruit of the cherry tree in a gold chalice, poisoned by our own stupidity, (c) divine opportunity to rise above the mere physical, or (d) none of the above.

Ian Anderson—flute and vocals for rock band Jethro Tull

Life is a world full of opportunities that have been recognized. A dirt road across a magnificent landscape that is full of drama, delight, and challenges. Along the way there will be loose gravel, soft sand, boulders and fallen trees, steep drop-offs, and river crossings. Life is learning the fun that comes from anticipating and planning for the things that could happen.

It is the moments of challenge that tell us who we really are and the growth of perspective. It is the kindness of others when we drop our bikes and a helping hand is there, and being able to be that helping hand. It is the smiles, laughter, and sense of achievement when we make it through each challenge. It is the stunning views and the discovery of things along the way that we had no idea existed. It is the moments we take to stop and really value what we are surrounded by, because each day should be full of moments, not the blur of the chase to the next goal.

Life? What does it mean? It means waking up to each day knowing that not everything is going to run smoothly, but being focused on all the wonderful opportunities that will be woven into each new day.

Sam Manicom—author of adventure motorcycle travel books

The meaning of life is the goal that we all seek along life's journey. This long—and sometimes short—road takes us past many births and deaths, loves, and lost loves. Life's events seem to fly by us like blades of grass along the road. Yet, in our struggles and adventures along this highway, we are but a speck of dust in the vast universe's scheme of things. You see, it is about how we conduct ourselves on this trip, so that at the end of the road the ride captain greets us with open arms and says: "Well done, my good and faithful servant."

David Burton—facilities services technician

The truest test of one's character is when things are going badly, not when it's all good.

Gary Vitti—retired Los Angeles Lakers head athletic trainer

Ride motorcycles and chase ladies . . . until they catch you. Life is a party, and always be happy you were invited. Sometimes life is tough and then you dance.

Jeremiah Gerbracht—actor

Old minds have memories.
Young minds have dreams.

Rande Gerber—bar and nightlife industry entrepreneur and
cofounder and partner (with friend George Clooney) of
Casamigos Tequila

Never water yourself down because someone can't handle you at 100 proof. Ride loud, ride proud.

Twanna Bedenbaugh—cable industry

Life has not been a simple trip. A terrific journey that's not easy, but definitely interesting. I learn something new every day. It can be as simple as a like or dislike, to something I have eaten, or to a tear on a person's face that has no answer for the reason why. So after many years on this journey, I can say, "be strong and don't take anything for granted." There is a spirit that guides every last one of us. Embrace it and live life to its fullest.

David Gordon—retired from motion picture industry

Jerilynn Stephens
Courtesy of Jerilynn Stephens

Dream big or don't bother.

Jerilynn Stephens—department head hairstylist of *The Voice*. Emmy-nominated and Guild Award–winning hairstylist

Procrastination is the assassination of motivation.

Ronald Anderson—mate and pilot merchant mariner

It is about being true to myself and remaining a person that has a moral compass that points true north. It is being able to lay my head on my pillow at night, knowing that at the end of the day I was honest, kind hearted, and empathetic toward my fellow humans, and that I challenged myself to strengthen my skills, continue to learn, stay young in heart, and not be judgmental toward anyone. It is not about acceptance or "attaboys." It is simply being the best that I can be to myself and those around me.

Renee Harrall—copublisher of *Thunder Roads Louisiana* magazine

The meaning of life is commitment. There is no magic wand to make it all come together. Having goals and working hard to succeed in all areas—personally, professionally, and in giving—and staying committed.

Rebecca Herwick—president and CEO of Global Products Inc.

Be true to yourself in all you do. For better or worse, own up to your actions, for they are the only ones you can control. Some will respect you; some won't. At the end of the day, when you lay your head to rest, only you can decide if you have done the best you can.

John Boivin—truck driver and member of the Hogs and Heroes Foundation

Life is all based on your character. Your reputation is who you are, how you go along in life, and how you make it. Whether you want to get to the top or to the bottom, it is just a wonderful world we live in, and you just have to get out there and experience it. If you don't, you are just going to fall behind.

Shaun Carroll Jr.—co-owner of ready-mix company

After sixty years of living life at full throttle, I have come to the understanding that it is both to learn from and teach others through our actions, words, and from our experiences that we have both lived through and, for some of us, survived. I think each of us goes through hard times that teach and test us, and those values that we hold true to our own view of the world and our place in it. The good times hold as much value as the bad. These truths are humility, wisdom, honor, valor, morals, ethics, and respect. I may have missed a few, but these I hold in high regard.

Each of us seeks our own sense of liberty, freedom, and a sense of self, knowing that someday it will be time to check out of this world. When that ride is over, I hope that we will have gone to our graves knowing that we have lived life to the fullest and earned our stripes with the light of knowledge that casts no shadows. If we did it even half right, then we will have helped others along the way.

Larry Phillips—founder and owner of Beast Custom Cycles

Always remember that we are on borrowed time; tomorrow is never promised. At the end of the day, you and only you are what you have. Learn to embrace and love yourself without restrictions. I am one that will not go to the grave wishing I would have, I could have, or I should have. I want no regrets in life, just adventures. Adventures make the greatest memories.

Jodi Gimse—international logistics order coordinator

Courtesy of Cameron Carbrey

CHAPTER NINE

BRING IT ON HOME

Life is our gift:

. . . to be lived to the fullest. To take it to the limit and push forward and beyond.

. . . to make sure we do not squander the gift and simply exist, but to truly live.

. . . to work hard, to play harder, and to learn to be aware that everything we do affects others.

. . . to leave behind a legacy.

. . . to take care of those who love us and to be an active part of the circle. The circle of love. The circle of respect. The circle of life.

The meaning of life can be looked at as we have but one life to live, and although there are no do-overs in life, we need to learn from our own mistakes and, we hope, become wise enough to learn from others.

We need to teach our children well and not crush them with fear, but nurture their dreams with empowerment. We need to encourage young people to follow their dreams and let nothing stand in their way, especially insecurity or self-doubt.

. . . to lead by example.

. . . to find what we love to do and make sure we do it. Find who we love and let them know it every day.

Life should be a conscious decision we make every day, rather than a desperate feeling that haunts us. We need to know that we are all just one second away from being in total control of our own lives.

Life is about:

. . . *living without fear, facing those fears head on, respecting them, and conquering them.*

. . . *never compromising our beliefs, but being smart enough to know when we have to make compromises.*

. . . *finding a balance where we enjoy our work and love our playtime. Where our responsibilities feel like an honor, rather than an obligation. Searching for this fearlessly.*

. . . *living for the moments where we feel the most, whether happy, angry, sad, or just the feeling all over our body when a song gives us chills, a movie makes us want to cry, or someone we love gives us that look that gets us all choked up.*

. . . *relishing true pleasure and rewarding ourselves, but never taking it for granted.*

. . . *achieving a sense of accomplishment coupled with humility.*

. . . *never settling for less than we know we deserve.*

. . . *having our eyes wide open and being willing to recognize the signs of everything around us that is in our life for an unknown reason.*

. . . *working hard to make sure that we are receptive and open to positive life energy and exchanging it with the universe, and always giving something back.*

. . . *gratitude and recognizing the good things we have been blessed with.*

. . . *never feeling like a victim.*

. . . *paving the roads to our own destinies.*

Lastly, and most importantly, life is about having dreams and goals, and never forgetting that ultimately life is the path we choose, a long, hard road that we live to ride and ride to live.

Evan Seinfeld—musician (founder of Biohazard) and actor (HBO prison drama *Oz*)

Evan Seinfeld
Courtesy of Jason Horne

Courtesy of Sturgis Buffalo Chip Campground

Life is about the connections you make along your journey, whether you are on two wheels or not. Our souls and spirits are shaped by the people we encounter every day. You have the freedom to choose how each interaction affects you and how you affect those around you—positively, negatively, or indifferently. You gotta spread the good stuff to get it back. Absorb knowledge from the bad stuff, radiate the kind of energy you want in your life, and let all the nonsense bounce off you. In the end, you alone have control of your life's journey. You never hand the keys to your motorcycle to just anyone, so don't let anyone take control of your spirit. Take every connection for what it's worth, and trust yourself.

Jennifer Baquial—industrial automation engineer and president of the Sirens Women's Motorcycle Club of NYC

Since I am in my midforties (the midpoint in life), I'm not sure that I fully understand everything there is to know about what the meaning life is as a whole. However, I do feel that I have learned some basic credos in the living I have done that have been a help to me and that I would like to pass on to others, especially my children. A few of my favorites are as follows:

Not everything and everyone are always what they appear to be.

This falls in line with the old saying "you can't judge a book by its cover." I do not put much stock in what people tell me, but I do pay a tremendous amount of attention to what people show me with their actions. I have been fooled so many times by trusting someone (based on their words) who really did not deserve to be trusted. If I had paid more attention to what they were doing, rather than what they were saying, I could have saved myself a lot of disappointment and grief. On the other hand, I have made the mistake of refusing someone or something only because of what I perceived that someone or something to be. By adopting opinions that were based solely on unfounded rumor and myth, I feel sure that I've cost myself some opportunities to know some people or learn something that possibly could have greatly enriched my life.

I have personally been characterized incorrectly and unfairly at times because of my "outlaw" persona in the music industry, which comes from exercising my right to make music my own individualized way. This approach to my music would cause some folks to automatically expect me to be difficult, arrogant, egotistical—a bad boy, etc.—if they were to meet me on the street. Anytime I hear about these unflattering descriptions of my personality, I just shake my head. I honestly believe that anyone who perceives me as being that way has probably never met me and certainly does not know me.

As the result of knowing how it feels to be inaccurately branded, I try very hard these days to do away with preconceived notions. Everything and everyone new in my life start with a clean slate. I try not to rush to judgments on anything or anybody. "Trust, but verify what you see for yourself" has been a credo that has served me well. I try to always keep an open mind. I keep both eyes wide open, too.

Mean what you say and say what you mean.

I'm a pretty plainspoken guy. I think so much time is wasted by people who want to dance around an issue rather than get to the heart of it. It is very frustrating to me to have my time wasted. I feel that my time is the most valuable thing I own, and there is so precious little of it. If someone has news for me that they feel I am not going to like, I still want to be given the news straight. No sugar coating. No presoftening. No hinting at or alluding to. Just lay it on me, and I'll deal with how I "feel about it" later. By the same token, I don't skirt around anyone's feelings when discussing any issue with anyone. I don't have time for it. If you don't really want to know what I think, don't ask me. While this approach has occasionally put me in hot water because it is far too direct for some, it is greatly admired and appreciated by others. One thing's for sure: if you practice this type of dialogue, folks will never have to wonder about where they stand with you. Wouldn't it be nice to have that kind of clarity from everyone we come in contact with?

Don't get too high on the highs or too low on the lows.

Speaking for me and anyone I have ever been able to relate to, life does not stagnate. I've been to funerals where I have heard the deceased sadly described as someone who "just got into a rut in their life that they never could get out of." I've never understood that terminology. Like anyone else, I have good days and bad. I have even experienced extended streaks in my life where almost everything I did and everything around me seemed to spiral. Sometimes it seemed to all spiral up, and other times it felt like the complete opposite. I think every life is filled with these ups and downs. I am really kind of glad that life isn't always the same. In my opinion, life would be too boring without contrast. I think the key to dealing with this ever-changing sea is maintaining an even keel. I enjoy the good times and good things that come my way in life, but I try not to overindulge myself in them, or fool myself into thinking that it will be nothing but good from here on out. While bad times and less desirable situations are not nearly as easy to deal with, I try to remind myself that everything happens for a reason and that "this too shall pass."

On an overall positive note, I like to think of all of life as a learning experience. We should feel honored to have the opportunity to pass along the things learned in life that might help make this world a better place for future generations.

Travis Tritt—Grammy Award-winning singer, songwriter, and musician

Travis Tritt
Courtesy of John Reasoner (R Photos)

The meaning of life to me, in my world, is no prejudice, no bullying, and accepting the things we can't change, courage to change the things we can, and the wisdom to know the difference.

I have worn many hats: actor, writer, radio personality, martial artist, and ordained minister. And a lot of things that I wanted to do, I did. Sure, I would have loved to be a baseball player or a law enforcement officer, but I went where the good Lord brought me. My talent for drumming brought me to being one of the top drummers in the world. There was a time where success had ended and I had to feed my family. I chose many different jobs outside of music and realized I could do anything I wanted to do.

Prejudice plays no part in my life. I have friends of all different races, backgrounds, and religions; they are all great people. Do not let a few screwed-up people ruin it for all. Treat everyone as you want to be treated. Remember, prejudice is not just measured by race, creed, or religion. I have tattoos, play in a rock band, look like a thug, and ride a motorcycle. Before people know me, they tend to shy away; however, when they get to know me, I am invited to their house for brunch. That's the way it is.

Bullying: No! No! No! We all have feelings. If you feel that you want to pick on someone because they look, act, or are different, no excuse. Accept and get to know them. You might be surprised, because they could be just like you. They are human beings just trying to live their life how they know it best.

Remember where you came from. Do not judge. Do charity work because you want to and not because of the mindset of "What's in it for me?" There are a lot of people who can't be bothered, and then there are a lot of people who remember when they were there. Give because it is the right thing to do, not to correct your sins. God is not fooled.

Enjoy life. Don't be stupid. Be positive and do positive things. The rest will be sorted out by karma.

A. J. Pero (1959–2015)—drummer in the heavy-metal band Twisted Sister

167

ACKNOWLEDGMENTS

Words fail to express my gratitude to all who have supported and encouraged me along the path to publishing *The Meaning of Life According to Bikers*. I thank my family and friends for your continued support, never once scoffing at my passion for the book's mission, even though most knew full well the hardships I endured during the decade-long "marathon" to get the book into the hands of readers.

The book could not exist without the generosity of spirit from the members of the motorcycle community who participated in the book. Whether I interviewed you on the road or contacted you via the world of celebrity or social media, you hold a special place in my heart for having the courage to help this geeky-ass "cager" shine a light on the charitable heart of your community. I will forever be grateful for the love and respect you offer, and will spend the last of my days upholding my promise to make you proud that you gave a leg up.

Much appreciation is given to the talented photographers who generously donated images to help create a visually stunning book. To those who work to support the celebrity and famous—agents, publicists, managers, and assistants—I send my heartfelt appreciation for your efforts. You were of immeasurable help, and I thank you so very much.

Special thanks is offered to my literary agent, Gordon Warnock of Fuse Literary, who stood alone in believing in the book's mission and invested many years to find a home for the book.

Lastly, to my unpaid editor and lifelong cheerleader, my mom, Yvonne Matherne. You continue to be the wind beneath my wings.

APPENDIX

Boot Campaign

The Boot Campaign mission is to promote patriotism for America and our military community, raise awareness of the unique challenges service members face during and post-service, and provide assistance to military personnel, past and present, and their families. www.bootcampaign.org/

Harley's Angels Cruzin' to Cure

The Mission of Harley's Angels is to promote breast cancer awareness and education, and to support research for the prevention and cure of breast cancer. Harley's Angels Cruzin' to Cure is a 501(c)3 nonprofit organization and is not affiliated with any dealer, manufacturer, or motorcycle enthusiast organization. With one out of eight women being diagnosed with breast cancer in their lifetime, it is no surprise that there are also several breast cancer survivors within our group. http://theharleysangels.org/

JP's Peace, Love and Happiness Foundation

John Paul DeJoria signed the Giving Pledge in 2011 as a formal promise to continue giving back. That same year, he founded JP's Peace, Love and Happiness Foundation to invest in charities that share the core values of his companies: sustainability, social responsibility, and animal friendliness. John Paul believes that success unshared is failure. To that end, the DeJoria family is committed to contributing to a sustainable planet through investing in people, protecting animals, and conserving the environment. http://peacelovehappinessfoundation.org/

Kiehl's LifeRide for amfAR

In 2010, Kiehl's introduced the Kiehl's LifeRide for amfAR, an annual motorcycle ride through major US cities that includes multiple high-profile events at Kiehl's stores along the way to raise consumer and media awareness about amfAR and the fight against AIDS. With the help of our friends, customers, and riders, by the end of the eighth annual LifeRide for amfAR, Kiehl's will have raised more than $150,000 in 2017, and more than $1,700,000 total for amfAR via motorcycle rides and event donations since 2010. www.amfar.org/liferide/

Kyle Petty Charity Ride Across America

One of the most successful and popular charity events in the country, this annual motorcycle trek engages celebrities, ride sponsors, motorcycle enthusiasts, fans, and local communities to raise funds and awareness for Victory Junction. Since 1995, more than 8,175 riders have logged 11.9 million cumulative motorcycle miles and raised more than $18 million for Victory Junction and other children's charities. www.kylepettycharityride.com/index.php

Love Ride Foundation

The Love Ride Foundation continues its successful history of forwarding charitable causes for underprivileged children and US veterans through sponsored events. During the last thirty-two years, the Love Ride Foundation has raised over $25 million for important local and national causes, including the Muscular Dystrophy Association, Wounded Warrior Project, and the USO. www.glendaleharley.com/

Motorcycle Charity Associates

Its mission is to produce and promote events sharing the common goal of supporting worthwhile 501(c)(3) charities in research, education, community programs, health services, and advocacy efforts. www.motorcyclecharityassociates.org/

Peace, Love and Happiness Charity Motorcycle Ride

The Peace, Love and Happiness Charity Motorcycle Ride was conceived in 2002, while two bikers (John Paul DeJoria and Gary Spellman) were riding through the Texas Hill Country. They created an event to help and support the families of fallen peace officers and any and all abused and neglected children. Since then, the event has gone on to support not only the 100 Club of Central Texas, but global causes as well, such as the Water Keepers Alliance. www.peacelovehappiness.com/

Ride4COPS

Ride4Cops was created by NIC CEO Harry Herington, who, as a former law enforcement officer, recognized the need to support the friends and families whom fallen officers leave behind. During his career in law enforcement, Harry remembered the promise he made to his partners: "If something happens to me, take care of my family." That promise continues to take place today across the country between thousands of law enforcement officers. www.ride4cops.com/ride4cops/index.html

Rock and Ride for the Cure

It is our mission to continue Bruce Panfil's charitable legacy with Rock and Ride for the Cure, uniting family and friends to raise money for pancreatic cancer research. Rock and Ride for the Cure is a nonprofit 501(c)(3) that is determined to help find a cure for pancreatic cancer. All proceeds from Rock and Ride for the Cure go to the Pancreas Center at the Columbia University Medical Center.

Rolling Thunder, Inc.

A class 501(c) (4) nonprofit organization with over ninety chartered chapters throughout the United States and members abroad. While many members of Rolling Thunder® Inc. are veterans, and many ride motorcycles, neither qualification is a prerequisite. Rolling Thunder® Inc. members are old and young, men and women, veterans and nonveterans. All are united in the cause to bring full accountability for the Prisoners of War / Missing in Action (POW/MIA) of all wars, reminding the government, the media, and the public with our watchwords: "We Will Not Forget." www.rollingthunder1.com/

Star Treatments

Founded by Matt DiRito, bassist for Pop Evil, Star Treatments assists families of children surviving cancer by taking care of transportation costs and needs to and from cancer treatment facilities. The child receives the "star treatment" on the way to their chemo treatments. http://startreatments.org/index.php

Sturgis Buffalo Chip and Legends Ride

The Sturgis Buffalo Chip® remains one of the world's most televised and longest-running independent music festivals. To date, the Buffalo Chip has donated nearly $600,000 to deserving charitable organizations, including Black Hills Special Olympics, Black Hills Children's Home, Sky Ranch for Boys, Sturgis Motorcycle Museum, Combat Wounded Coalition, America's Mighty Warriors, Lakota Heritage, and educational scholarships through the Buffalo Chip

Challenge program. The Sturgis Buffalo Chip's Legends Ride is dedicated to bringing rally goers together to raise significant funds for local charities and the Buffalo Chip Challenge Scholarship Program. Having raised more than $500,000 for charity since its inception in 2008, the Legends Ride has played host to some of the biggest names in television, film, music, and motorcycling, along with riders from all corners of the world. www.buffalochip.com/

The Bob & Renee Parsons Foundation

The Bob & Renee Parsons Foundation was established in February 2012, with the hope to change the lives of our country's critically wounded veterans and to improve outcomes for individuals and families living in poverty. Founded by serial entrepreneur Bob Parsons and business executive Renee Parsons, the foundation is guided by the couple's personal experiences, values, and beliefs. www.tbrpf.org/

GoDaddy

GoDaddy believes that its responsibility as a corporate citizen is to make a difference in the communities in which it operates. As part of that philosophy, GoDaddy contributes to nonprofit organizations that focus on causes that are meaningful to our business, our customers, our employees, and our community. Since 2002, GoDaddy has donated more than $15 million to a variety of charitable organizations. GoDaddy understands that giving back to the community is not accomplished just with money and resources, but also with talent and time. www.GoDaddyCares.com

The General Tommy Franks Leadership Institute and Museum

Invests in the nation's future leaders through several education and outreach programs, including our Mobile Classroom + Road Show, which enriches and enhances the learning experience for students by bringing the GTFLIM to their location. www.tommyfranksmuseum.org/

The Miracle Ride Foundation

The Miracle Ride is one of the nation's largest and longest-running motorcycle charity events. We are made up of a board, a director, more than 250 volunteers, and thousands of Miracle Riders who are street and off-road motorcyclists, all of whom share a great passion for keeping kids healthy. We are riders who prove that "Hope Happens When We Ride." The Miracle Ride Foundation, Inc., a 501(c)3 nonprofit organization, believes that helping fund Riley Hospital for Children is the best way to demonstrate that shared belief. Since 1994, the Miracle Ride has donated more than $6.2 million to Riley Children's Hospital. The Miracle Ride and Riley Hospital are in Indiana. www.miracleride.net

Two Wheels for Life
Established to continue the wonderful fundraising events within the world of motorcycles, such as Day of Champions. Funds that are raised continue to support Riders for Health International and programs in Africa, helping them reach remote rural communities with life-saving health care. www.twowheelsforlife.org.uk/

Veterans Charity Ride
A year-round nonprofit program specifically designed to assist wounded and amputee combat veterans with the needs and issues they deal with on a daily basis. Helping our veterans through outreach, action, follow-up, and activities is what drives our organization. http://veteranscharityride.org/

Louise Lewis has more than 30 years of experience in marketing and advertising, having held senior-level positions on the client, advertising agency, and advertising sales sides of the business. She considers herself a self-growth junkie, continuing to seek light, love, and wisdom in her daily life. She has been a volunteer for Big Brother/Sister, Catholic Ministries Juvenile Detention, and CHOC Children's Hospital, and has devoted more than a decade to her meaning-of-life journey with her "biker dude" friends, as the hospital kids call them. She was born and raised in Louisiana, obtained a degree in communications from California State University, Fullerton, and now cares for her mom in Florida.

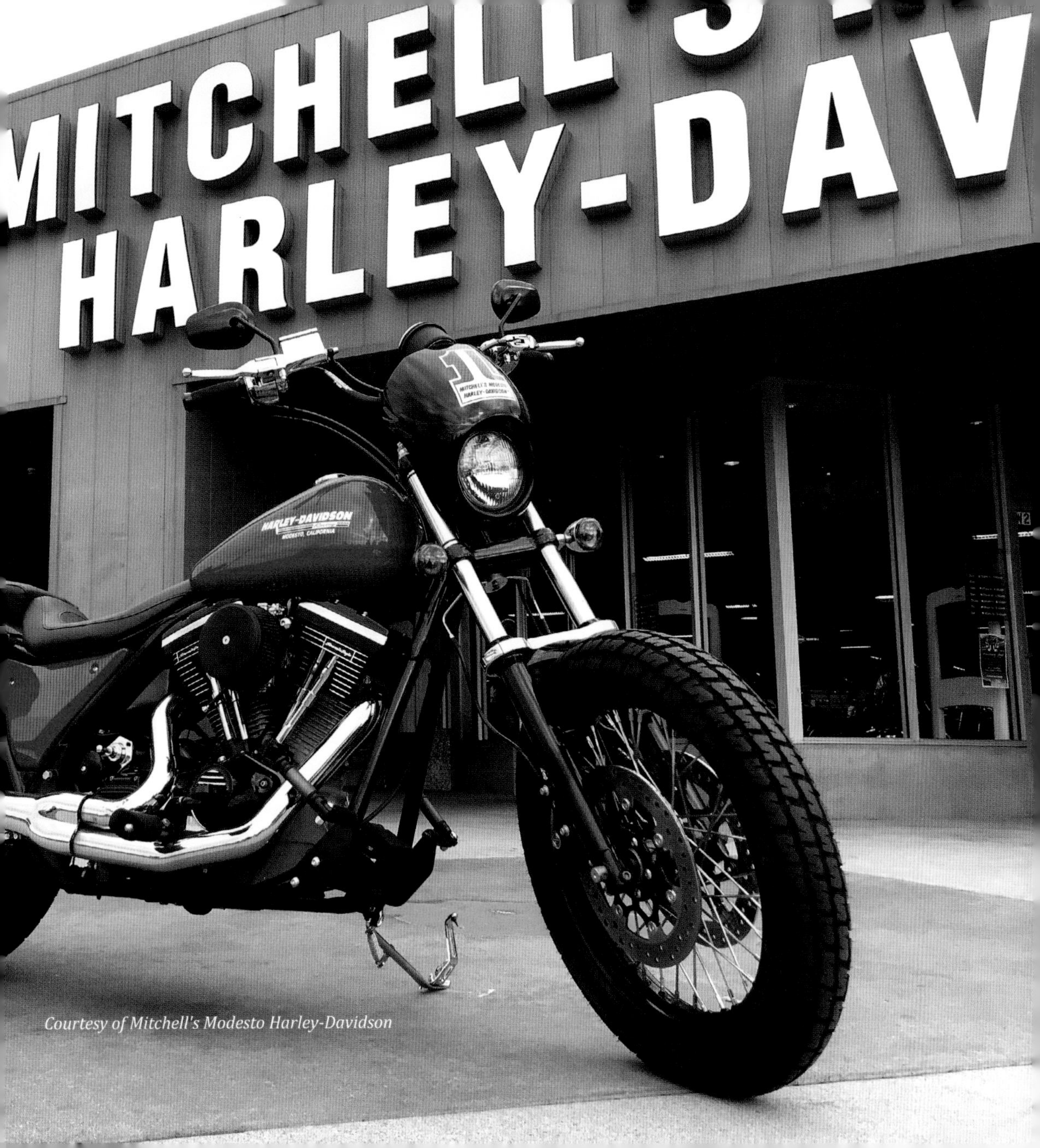

Courtesy of Mitchell's Modesto Harley-Davidson

Designed by Molly Shields
Cover design by Mathew Goodman
Cover image courtesy of Paul Contreras, Beyond Photos Photography, Rio Rancho, New Mexico
Type set in URWWoodTypD/ConduitOSITC

ISBN: 978-0-7643-5596-7
Printed in China

Published by Schiffer Publishing, Ltd.
4880 Lower Valley Road
Atglen, PA 19310
Phone: (610) 593-1777; Fax: (610) 593-2002
E-mail: Info@schifferbooks.com
Web: www.schifferbooks.com

For our complete selection of fine books on this and related subjects, please visit our website at www.schifferbooks.com. You may also write for a free catalog.

Schiffer Publishing's titles are available at special discounts for bulk purchases for sales promotions or premiums. Special editions, including personalized covers, corporate imprints, and excerpts, can be created in large quantities for special needs. For more information, contact the publisher.

We are always looking for people to write books on new and related subjects. If you have an idea for a book, please contact us at proposals@schifferbooks.com.